Roots, Rocks and Rain
Native Trees of the Florida Keys

Robin Robinson
Key West Citizen Columnist
for the
Key West Garden Club

Published by Sora Publishing

Sora Publishing
1800 Atlantic Boulevard, A-405
Key West, Florida 33040
U.S.A.

sorapublishing@comcast.net

keywestgardenclub.com

Library of Congress Cataloging-in-Publication Data
Robinson, Robin 1943-
Roots, rocks, rain: native trees of the florida keys / By Robin Robinson
Library of Congress Control Number: 2011908415
Plants on the cover: Cinnamon Bark, Sweet Acacia, Fiddlewood, Jamaica Caper

ISBN 9780976575641
includes index

SAN 256-4157

Cover design by Nathalie Breakstone
Photo Credits: All photos by author

Although such information is reported in the historical literature and in other sources, the author makes no representation or claims as to the accuracy, usefulness or viability of the Native American and other health or food uses of the plants and their products described herein. Such descriptions are for historical and entertainment references only and for no other purpose. No suggestion is made, nor intended, for the use of any plants or their products not certified by properly qualified medical or government authority. The ingestion of any plant or its products not tested and certified by proper governmental authority such as the U.S. Food and Drug Administration or the U.S. Department of Agriculture may cause detrimental health effects, including serious illness and death. It is not recommended.

Table of Contents

Blackbead *(Pithecillobium keyense)*   4

Black Ironwood *(Krugiodendron ferreum)*   6

Black Mangrove *(Avicennia germinans)*   8

Blolly (*Guapira discolor*)   10

Buttonwood, Green *(Conocarpus erectus)*   12

         Silver *(C. erectus var. sericeus)*

Cinnamon Bark *(Canella winterana)*   14

False Mastic *(Sideroxylon foetidissimum)*   16

Fiddlewood (*Citharexylum spinosum*)   18

Geiger Tree (*Cordia sebestena*)   20

Gumbo-limbo *(Bursera simaruba)*   22

Inkwood *(Exothea paniculata)*   24

Jamaica Caper *(Capparis cynophallophora)*   26

Jamaica Dogwood *(Piscidia piscipula)*   28

Joewood *(Jacquinia keyensis)*   30

Lignum vitae *(Guaiacum sanctum)*   32

Mahogany *(Swietenia mahagoni)*   34

Milkbark *(Drypetes diversifolia)*   36

Myrsine *(Rapanea punctata)*   38

Oysterwood *(Gymnanthes lucida)*   40

Paradise Tree *(Simarouba glauca)*   42

Pigeon Plum Tree *(Coccolobo diversifolia)*   44

Poisonwood Tree *(Metopium toxiferum)*   46

Red Mangrove *(Rhizophora mangle)*   48

Satinleaf *(Chrysophylium oliviforme)*   50

Seagrape *(Coccoloba uvifera)*   52

Seven-year Apple *(Genipa clusiifolia)*   54

Smooth Strongback (*Bourreria succulenta*)   56

Soapberry *(Sapindus saponaria)*   58

Spanish Stopper (*Eugenia foetida*)   60

Spicewood Tree (*Calyptranthes pallens*)   62

Strangler Fig *(Ficus aurea)*   64

Sweet Acacia *(Acacia farnesiana)*   66

White Mangrove *(Languncularia racemosa)*   68

Wild Dilly *(Manikara bahamensis)*   70

Wild Lime *(Zanthoxylum fagara)*   72

Wild Tamarind (*Lysiloma latisiliquum*)   74

Willow Bustic (*Sideroxylon salicifolium*)   76

Index

Scientific and Common Names   77

Acknowledgements   78

About the Author   79

Quick Order Form   80

Blackbead *(Pithecellobium keyense)*

Bring Back Miami Blue Butterflies – Plant Blackbead

The Keys blackbead tree *(Pithecellobium keyense)* is a small native species that grows in the understory of hardwood hammocks and was recently removed from the threatened list. According to the Champion Trees list in the Division of Forestry, the largest specimen, located in Monroe County, is only 13 feet high, 15 inches in circumference and has a spread of 15 feet. It is wider than it is tall.

Think of yourself as a small wood-sprite crawling in the dark labyrinth of the branches. The branches of this small tree are dark, twisty and mysterious. Bark is dark gray with shallow fissures, just enough to hold on to as you hoist yourself into its heights.

The leaves emerge from short stems and terminate in opposite linear leaves; two or three sets of leaflets grace each stem. New leaf growth is pinkish.

The flowers are glorious pink or white one-inch globes, each filament tipped with golden yellow. They burst into bloom throughout the year and saturate the air with a fabulous aroma drawing insects to the plant. Butterflies especially love the nectar. Cassius blue (*Leptotes cassius,*) Florida duskywing (*Ephyriades brunneus,*) Florida white (*Appias drusilla,*) giant swallowtail (*Papilio cresphontes,*) great southern white (*Ascia monuste,*) five different kinds of skippers and other butterflies feed on this ecologically valuable tree.

It is the larval host plant for cassius blue *(Leptotes cassius)* and large orange sulphur (*Phoebis agarithe.*) It does its job for these butterflies, but the butterfly on the top on the list is the Miami blue. Tom Wilmer, Katie Lyons and Paula Cannon's reported in the *Key West Citizen* on Jan. 15, 2010, that there was a large colony of Miami blue butterflies on Boca Grande Key.

The Miami blue is a rare species that was thought to be extirpated from the Florida Keys. Then they were found in Bahia Honda State Park, only to disappear again after the cold spell of 2010. A population of 40 butterflies was released in areas where they were thought to thrive, such as in the Key West Botanical Gardens, but they did not do well in any of these areas.

Cannon observed them laying eggs on the buds of the blackbead tree. In December, 2009, Cannon decided to explore other offshore islands and headed for the Marquesas about 15 miles from Boca Grande.

"I was not there ten minutes when I sighted my first Miami blue." Cannon continued on to the Marquesas and visited several other islands. She found a total of seven islands that had Miami blues.

"Clearly it was the dominant butterfly species on the Marquesas Islands. The Miami blues were both ovipositing (laying eggs) and nectaring on the lush pink or white flowers of the blackbead trees."

The blackbead tree pops a splendid thin fruit pod, four to five inches long. Because of the pod's narrow curved shape, this plant has been called monkey earrings or ram's horn. Inside the reddish-brown pod are black seeds with a sweet red aril. Birds eat the red aril that is attached to the quarter-inch black seed. They swallow the seed and fly off to deposit it elsewhere.

It provides a home for gall wasps. Blackbead can withstand short periods of flooding, drought and salt wind. It likes full sun and well-drained nutrient-poor soils. Blackbead, an undistinguished citizen of the hammock, is a key element.

Black Ironwood (*Krugiodendron ferreum*)

Ironwood's Weighty Issues

Two thousand one hundred years ago, Archimedes popped out of the bathtub, shouted, "Eureka, I have found it!" and in his excitement ran naked through the streets. His bathtub discovery of specific gravity put black ironwood on the top of the heavy tree heap.

The ironwood tree is a much better behaved tree than the naked Archimedes, maybe because of its weightiness in the world. Put this wood in water and it straight away sinks to the bottom. Sometimes it is called leadwood for this reason. While Archimedes discovered that one gram of water has a specific gravity of 1.0 and occupies one centimeter, the ironwood has a specific gravity of 1.42. It is the densest wood in North America and weighs 80 pounds per cubic foot. Lignum vitae's specific gravity is 1.39; balsa wood is 0.17. Ironwood takes its position at the weighty top seriously and grows slowly, taking many years to get to its full height.

Our ancestors made fence posts, axe handles, cogs and rollers, cross ties and mallets from the wood. It burns slowly and evenly and was often used as firewood. I can imagine that the wood is difficult to cut with an ax, as another name for the tree is musclewood. If sawed, it smells like molten lead. The Mayans made it into bows, arrows and lances. Indigenous Indians used the bark and root as a mouthwash to relieve tooth and gum ailments. In the Bahamas, they used the fruit to make jams and wine. In the Keys it has no known commercial value.

The tree has a narrow trunk four to ten inches in diameter. The bark is gray and as it ages, forms long vertical ridges. Its inch-and-a-half long leaves are an attractive dark green and glossy. A female cutter bee takes perfect circles out of the oval leaves, then stuffs the leaf tissue into a hole and lays an egg. She continues to do this until she creates a long, cylindrical grouping of leaves stuffed one inside the other each with an egg in between. When the larvae hatch, they feed on the leaves.

The flower is small and greenish, but has copious amounts of nectar that attract all manner of insects, butterflies and moths. It blooms year round, but more so in the spring and summer.

The round fruits are small and black when ripe in the fall. They are edible and are quite sweet. Birds and other animals love them and perch in the trees while they eat.

The orderly tree grows in the interior of hardwood hammocks growing up to twenty feet in height and ten feet in width in full sun or part shade. Once established, it is moderately salt, drought and high wind tolerant, which makes it a good xeriscaping tree for the Keys. It has the unusual ability to quiver in high winds.

A patient gardener is needed to grow this tree from seed.

This is a good tree as an under-story plant. Its moderate growth may be an advantage, as it does not need trimming. As a native, it has no serious diseases to mar its beauty. Plant it where you can lie underneath it to gaze through its canopy made lacy by the cutter bees.

The German botanist who named this tree was Ignatz Urban, an urbane man of the woods. He found it in Puerto Rico and called it Krug after the then German Counsel. *Dendron means* tree so the moniker is Krug's tree, sure to endear Urban to the government. The second word in the name, *ferreum*, means iron-like. He classified it in the Rhamnaceae Family.

You can see this tree at the Key West Garden Club. The tree is widely cultivated and available in plant nurseries.

Black Mangrove (Avicennia germinans)

Marvel at the Seeds and Roots of the Black Mangrove

It is amazing that any plant can survive living in salt water, but adaptation thrives in difficult circumstances. That is why the black mangrove (*Avicennia germinans*) is adapted to growing in the intertidal zone and does not like to be inundated with brackish water for long periods of time. This mangrove has developed a series of pencil-like roots called pneumatophores that grow from its long, underground roots. These roots protrude from the base of the tree and serve as breathing tubes for the tree, providing air through their pores for the roots.

The tree also has developed a system for survival that involves being able to expel salt crystals through glands in its leaves. A crust of salt forms on the topside of the leaf and is washed off with rains. A black mangrove is dependent on fresh water run-off to maintain optimum levels of salinity, but can eliminate 90% of the salt it takes into its roots.

A lima bean sized, green seedling ripens and sprouts while it is still on the parent tree. The name *germinans* refers to this process. When a propagule (seedling) finds a piece of moist ground it shoots down roots. Black mangrove forests cover the world's subtropical shorelines because the seedling of a mangrove can survive indefinitely in salt water, floating with the currents around the world.

The tree grows to 20 feet in height. The further north the tree exists, the smaller and bushier it gets. It does not survive frost. It has heavily furrowed, dark brown bark. When it falls off, the inner bark is orange. Its soil needs to be moist. It does not survive droughts well.

The leaves of a black mangrove are shiny, dark green on the top and hairy and silvery on the bottom and grow opposite each other. They are elliptical and grow profusely on the branches. The leaves are a larval host plant for the mangrove buckeye butterfly (*Junovia evarete*). When the leaves fall to the ground or water, they decompose. Fungi and microorganisms create food for a variety of marine life.

It gets tiny, white flowers year-round, although most heavily in June and July. Bees adore these blossoms, pollinating them readily. Black mangrove honey is delicious. The flowers are a nectar plant for the great southern white butterfly (*Ascia monuste.*)

The black mangrove is an ecological marvel. It provides stability for low-lying coasts and protection for shrimp, crabs and small fish. Most of Florida's game fish and commercial fish use the mangrove ecosystem as a breeding ground. The spotted mangrove crab and several snails nibble on the propagules. Various crabs consume the leaves. Birds roost and nest in its branches. It is a feeding and breeding nursery.

The black mangrove is usually found between the red mangrove (*Rhizophora* mangle) and the white mangrove (*Laguncularia racemosa.*) The red mangrove stands directly in water. Although the black mangrove can withstand having its roots in salt water, it prefers a bit dryer land. The white mangrove grows even further back from the shoreline. Although all of these trees are called mangrove, they are not related to each other. They have in common that their seedlings germinate on the parent tree.

Unusually, the black heartwood of this mangrove is harder than the brown and yellow sapwood. The wood is oily and dense and not worked easily. The tree has been used for charcoal, marine construction and tanning leather. Tea prepared from the bark was used to treat ulcers, hemorrhoids, diarrhea, tumors and rheumatism. The fruit made a good insect repellant.

In Key West, a black mangrove may be seen on the Berg Nature Preserve at 1700 Atlantic Boulevard. It is also on Wisteria Island viewable from a boat. The tree photographed here is near Mud Key Creek. Take a boat ride through the Ten Thousand Islands around Everglades City that contains the largest concentration of the black mangrove in Florida.

Blolly, Beeftree (*Guapira discolor*)

Birds and Bees Hobnob in Thickets of the Blolly

Give us your poor, your tired, your winged travelers. Let them feast on the longleaf blolly or beeftree *(Guapira discolor)* as they migrate through our islands. Immigration is difficult for these free spirits winging their way northward. Ninety-miles is a considerable challenge when you are airborne, and you might need a rest and some chow when you arrive.

A variety of birds wing straight for the hearty, adaptable, beachfront blollys. Blollys are a small tree with a round crown and stout trunks commonly found in pine rockland and coastal berm habitats. Their two-inch-long, round-ended leaves are thin as they open and then thicken. They're light green and smooth on the top. The young branches droop from the tree when growing. Aqua-green lichens crawl all over the smooth gray trunks. When you find the lichens, it's another clue that you have found a blolly.

The tree shoots up quickly to 18 feet in height and as wide if left with multiple trunks, though it can be trained into a single trunk. However, there is a reason for the multiple trunks. Blolly is also known as antwood because it will sacrifice one of its trunks to ants. This is an important symbiotic relationship, because it provides habitat for the ant colony, and the ants' waste material helps to add fertilizer for the tree, a good reason to leave multiple trunks.

Blolly fills out after growing up. It likes moisture filled soil; however there is one growing on the beach near the Berg Nature Preserve growing in coral and sand that survived all the hurricanes of the last ten years. It tolerates salt spray, wind and does moderately well with drought. It will grow in full sun or light shade.

Male and female flowers occur on separate trees. They aren't much to look at, small and yellow-green but they make up for it by blooming year-round. The bees and butterflies seem to find them quite tasty. They are wind and insect pollinated.

The fruit is the real prize for our wing-flapping friends. If the tree is female, the blolly drips bright red drupes from the branches. Luscious, tantalizing berries attract fruit-eating tanagers, catbirds, and warblers. The ripening crop attracts insects, as a result, gray gnatcatchers, American redstarts and other insect-eating birds descend on the tree to eat the insects that are eating the fruit. A tree full of berries and wildlife is a magnificent sight. Regrettably, iguanas like the fruits, too.

Like the birds flying from other countries to our island shores, the word blolly comes from across the Atlantic Ocean. In England, a loblolly is a thicket that tends to grow in moist depressions. From there, comes the common name blolly, because of the trees, propensity to grow in close proximity to each other. The botanist J. F. Aublet took the scientific name, *Guapira,* from indigenous words meaning to eat and bitter. *Discolor* refers to the two surfaces of the leaf being unlike in color.

Although they have a symbiotic relationship to many insects, blollys are resistant to diseases and have few pests. They are propagated easily from seed. They can be ordered and purchased inexpensively from local nurseries.

Examples can be found at the Key West Garden Club. If you like to sit on your porch and watch the "homeless, tempest-tost" aviary travelers arrive on our golden shores, you can't get a better back yard tree than the blolly. (With apologies to Emma Lazarus.)

Green Buttonwood *(Conocarpus erectus L.)*
Silver Buttonwood *(Conocarpus erectus L. var. sericeus)*

The Honorable Key West Buttonwood

Key West's green buttonwood tree known as the scary tree, on the corner of Leon and Washington Street is the largest buttonwood in town. Stop by the corner and you will be amazed at the size of the trunk, the twists of the branches and the spread of the crown. This tree has seen many, many hurricanes. Denise Marchant, who owns the buttonwood's home, said that it has been much the same shape for the 46 years that her family has owned the house.

Buttonwood trees have hard, dense wood and do not have growth rings to determine age but this one looks like it is hundreds of years old.

The tree is considered native, being here before the 1600s. However, Janice Duquesnel from the Florida Department of Environmental Protection/Florida Park Service introduced me to a new method of determining whether a tree is native or not. She states that a tree is native if it arrived in the Keys naturally and was not brought here and planted by humans.

From looking at the two trees you wouldn't think that green and silver buttonwood trees were the same species. The green buttonwood has shiny dark green leaves, whereas the silver buttonwood has silver-gray leaves that are covered with a mat of silky hairs. The green buttonwood trees can grow to 30 feet while the silver ones generally remain smaller at 25 feet.

Buttonwoods live in nutrient-poor, well-drained soil, tolerate high salt winds, do not need additional watering and love the hot sun. The glands at the base of the leaf are nectar glands and not salt glands. There are also glands along the midrib where the veins meet the midrib. These are called domatia or air pockets and oftentimes have tiny mites living in the spaces. They have tiny bursts of flowers all year long, but peak in the summer.

Picturesque and contorted when planted near the ocean winds; they can grow right behind the mangrove layer near the beaches and in coastal swamps. Planted inland, they grow more symmetrically. They exist only below the freeze line in North America because they hate the cold but also grow as far away as the Galapagos and Western Africa. The small round brown seeds float, so seed clusters can make it all the way across oceans while retaining their vitality.

They do well as street trees, and there are some nice specimens planted in the median on Flagler Avenue in Key West. The versatile buttonwoods can be pruned into a four-foot hedge or allowed to grow into a handsome single trunk, 30-foot, vase-shaped tree.

Buttonwoods can take flooding, but they don't like to sit directly in the water for long periods of time. This is evident in the Kitso and Berg Nature Preserves on Atlantic Boulevard where many interior buttonwoods are dead. They grow best at about ten feet above sea level.

Some think that the common name comes from the round shape of the fruits that look like buttons, but buttons were actually made out of the hard wood of the tree. The bark of buttonwoods is high in tannin and has been harvested commercially for that use. The wood makes high-grade charcoal and is desirable for smoking meats and fish as it burns hot and slow. Bonsai enthusiasts love the silver trees and search for small plants around the roots in areas where a freeze has destroyed the mother plant.

The buttonwoods are important hosts for air plants and are particularly good for orchids and bromeliads. Tantalus martial (*Strymon martialis,*) amethyst hairstreaks *(Atlides halesus)* and Tantalus sphinx moths *(Aellopos tantalus)* use the tree both as larval host plant and for nectar. Sooty mold can attack the leaves, especially away from the coast, but it does not harm the tree.

Bravo to a buttonwood that is undaunted by the forces of nature and tenaciously lives through difficult times. This is one tough tree. Two shapes of silver buttonwood can be seen at the Key West Garden Club and across the street.

Cinnamon Bark *(Canella winterana)*

Inhale Cinnamon Bark's Spicy Aroma

The native cinnamon bark tree *(Canella winterana)* exudes the pleasant smell of its namesake. The Latin *canella* means cane referring to the form of cinnamon that rolls into a spiral, not to this tree's thin bark. The name *winterana* comes from another misnomer. William Winter was a famed botanist who had a tree named after him that was confused with cinnamon bark for a time.

The tree is an understory tree that grows to a height of 20 feet. It is usually taller than it is broad. It can grow in shade, but flowers more when it is in the sun. It has gray scaly bark on a narrow trunk. The dark-brown wood is heavy, hard and narrowly grained. It was used to make agricultural instruments, poles and charcoal. It has a specific gravity of 0.989 with a cubic foot weighing in at 61.7 pounds.

The alternate, simple, dark-green ovate leaves are thick and when crushed smell like cinnamon. The leaves also have a peppery taste when touched to the tongue. They are two to five inches long and one to two inches wide. Although it is endangered here in the Keys because of loss of habitat, it exists throughout the Caribbean and Mexico. It grows to 50 feet in Jamaica's rich soils.

The flowers are showy clusters with green buds turning to purple. Red flowers pop out at various times so that you see both buds and flowers at the same time. It flowers and seeds year round with fruit beginning a soft and fleshy red, then turning black.

Cinnamon bark likes our soil, can be inundated with brackish salt water and withstands salt wind, but it is usually protected by other vegetation.

The early explorers of the Caribbean noticed it. In January 1494, Diego Alverez Chanca, a physician traveling with Christopher Columbus wrote in a letter, "We found there a tree whose leaf had the finest smell of cloves that I have ever met with; it was like a laurel leaf, but not so large: but I think it was a species of laurel."

In folk medicine, the aromatic bark and leaves are used to relieve many symptoms of diseases, including headaches. The bark and leaves are also anti-fungal and anti-microbial. The outer bark is toxic and natives threw branches in the water to stun fish and make them easy to catch. The leaves contain the chemical myrcene, an essential oil used in the perfume industry.

Cinnamon bark is a nectar plant that feeds the rare Schaus' swallowtail butterfly *(Papilo aristodemus ponceanus,)* a three-and-three-fourths-inch black and yellow denizen of the air. These butterflies are federally listed as endangered. After Hurricane Georges only a few dozen were left. Their numbers rose to the low hundreds but were decimated again by the cold in 2010. Some birds that like the fruit of the cinnamon bark also eat the caterpillars and take a big toll from their recovering population every year. Various government and non-government organizations are studying them. Many popular birds thrive on a diet of cinnamon bark fruit.

You can see these trees near the turtle pond in the McCoy Indigenous Park or at the Key West Botanical Gardens on Stock Island.

False Mastic *(Sideroxylon foetidissimum)*

False Mastic Flowers Smell like Rotten Cheese

False Mastic *(Sideroxylon foetidissimum)* towers above the dry forests at 40 feet in height. The trunks are up to three feet wide and have buttresses at the bottom. The distinctive gray bark has large flakes that break off exposing the lovely orange inner bark. It is a member of the Sapotaceae Family and has some of its gummy latex characteristics.

The opposite and elliptic leaves are light to dark green about five inches long and two inches wide with a rippled edge. They cluster near the ends of the branches.

Small greenish-yellow flowers with five petals form in dense clusters on old stems. They soon give way to inch-long yellow-orange berries. As the berries fall to the ground they provide food for wildlife and make a gooey mess on the ground. The inch-long gummy fruit is tasty, but will make your lips stick together.

The threatened white-crowned pigeon *(Patagioenas leucocephala)* is attracted to the fruit of the false mastic tree and other natives. The mating partners form a strong bond during egg laying and incubation. When nesting, the males tend to stay with the nest during the day while the females feed, then the females incubate at night while the males feed. Both feed their pink fuzzy baby birds with crop milk which they produce in their throats and which contains the same proteins, fats and sugars as mammal milk.

16

The name of the tree is derived from the Latin word *foelidus*. We get our English word fetid from the same source. It means bad smelling. In fact, the name *foetidissimum* means especially bad smelling. The flowers stink like pungent, rotten cheese.

The tree grows well in moist well-drained soils and, as a tree located higher in the hammock, does not tolerate long-term flooding by brackish water. It has high drought and salt wind tolerance.

The tree attracts the false mastic psylla *(Ceropsylla sideroxyli,)* a jumping plant louse. Damage is often severe, but is part of a natural cycle. No treatment for the infestation is known.

The beautiful hard yellow and orange wood of the false mastic tree was highly desired for ship-building and cabinet-making in the West Indies. It was used in heavy and light construction and for agricultural implements.

False mastic trees grow half way up Florida mainly along the coasts with fewer of them in the middle and lower Keys. I have one that is 40 feet in height outside my balcony in Key West. There is another one in the Key West Tropical Forest and Botanical Gardens.

It is said, that when a member of the tribe was being extremely irritating, the Miccosukee Indians would rub the offender with the ashes of the false mastic tree in a body cleansing ritual to change the offensive attitude. I know a few people I'd like to send to that tribe for a little "cleansing with the ashes" ritual.

Fiddlewood (*Citharexylum spinosum*)

Fiddle-Faddle under the Fiddlewood

Last year, I planted a two-foot fiddlewood tree (*Citharexylum spinosum*) not knowing exactly what would transpire. One year later, this multi-stemmed bush has grown four feet and is giving me come hither looks and showing off its glossy, dark-green leaves with four inch long bracts of small, white five-petal flowers. It perfumes the air with the smell of lilacs. This is a plant that attracts lovers. "A loaf of bread, a jug of wine and thou, —And wilderness is Paradise now." (Omar Khayyam)

Our paradise should have more of these romantic specimens. The State of Florida thinks so, as it recommends the native fiddlewood tree (Verbenaceae Family) as an "outstanding ornamental tree that should be planted more."

When I first planted this tree I thought it would have a trunk. However, it took a bushy form that can be twenty feet high and twelve feet wide. Mine grew from two to six feet tall in one year even in our poor, alkaline soil. It is drought and salt soil tolerant. It flowers prolifically in the sun, but can also grow in light shade as it is a hammock species. It is also dioecious which means male and female flowers are found on separate trees.

Round, three-eighth-inch fruit form on the trees, at the same time as new flowers, in an orange drupe that eventually turns brown. The fruits are edible, sweet and juicy, but the two seeds take up most of the space, and there is not much pulp. The tree can be grown from these seeds. Plants grown from seeds are generally more genetically diversified and stronger. The dense, evergreen leaves are two to five inches long with a square, orange stalk and mid-rib. In the spring the leaves turn a showy orange before being shed. The trunk is brown and furrows with age.

Fiddlewood makes a great hedge and is so sturdy that it is recommended for parking lots and highways. Plant it by a window or a walkway so the smells can entice you. It is remarkably hearty and has few major diseases or pests. Sometimes moth caterpillars eat its leaves, but the caterpillars have no long-term effect on the plant. It is easily pruned and, if cut to the ground, will re-grow. Sounds hurricane-resistant to me.

Songbirds love the seeds. Hummingbirds, bees and butterflies, especially the ruddy daggerwing *(Marpesia petreus)* love the nectar. Listen up and you can hear "The buzzin' of the bees in the fiddlewood trees."

Fiddlewood comes from the West Indies and is considered native in the Keys. Its name, *Citharexylum*, means lyre from the Greek word *Kithara* and wood from the Greek, *xylon*. Not surprisingly, the wood has been used in the Caribbean to make the sounding boards of string instruments, hence, fiddle wood. The heavy, hard wood also is used to make cabinets. An example of fiddlewood that has been pruned to be a tree can be found at the Key West Tropical Forest and Botanical Gardens.

So don't fiddle-faddle. Plant this inexpensive tree in your garden. When you buy it, notice how many trunks it has to determine whether, in its soul, it wants to be a bush or a tree. It can be seen at the Key West Garden Club.

Geiger Tree (*Cordia sebestena*)

Flashy Orange Blossoms Grace the Geiger Tree

In the spring, birders stop to gape at the flamboyant Geiger tree (*Cordia sebestena*) that still stands in front of the Audubon House on Whitehead Street as they remember the white-crowned pigeons Audubon painted in its branches in 1832. (Actually his assistant painted the tree section.) If they are lucky, they get to see the threatened pigeons which Bill Merritt, Operations Manager at the Audubon House, says still visit every spring.

The Geiger tree has great smelling, three inch, white fruit, but Merritt says the pigeons prefer fig and poisonwood fruit. The Geiger fruit is not very tasty, but people who have eaten the seed kernels say they taste like filberts. The seeds can be propagated and sometimes seedlings pop up underneath the mother tree.

Audubon described the original tree as "fifteen feet high with a trunk of five inches." The tree is now 30 feet tall and has a trunk with a circumference of 51 inches. It could be well over 176 years old. How's that for hurricane survival? However, any tree could succumb to a large enough hurricane. Although named after the Key West wrecker, Captain John H. Geiger whose yard contained the tree, according to recent archeological findings, the Geiger tree existed in Florida long before the Europeans came. Roger L. Hammer says it *might* have floated here as the seeds are buoyant, but he believes that Geiger planted this particular one.

Huge orange blossoms flower on evergreen leaves are as large as a man's hand. If there is a drought, the trees will drop their leaves to conserve energy and help their survival. The trees bloom profusely all year when young and less frequently when older. They don't care a whit what their soil is like and wade right through saltwater floods. Early settlers used the rough textured leaves as sandpaper to smooth tortoise shells. In full sun, they grow at a moderate rate to reach 25 feet by 20 feet.

A group of botanists from Connecticut College watched a Geiger tree in the Caribbean for 5.3 hours and recorded 191 visits by hummingbirds to the bright orange flowers. (There *are* people like that.) The nectar also attracts butterflies and bees and is the nectar plant for the orange sulphur butterfly *(Phoebis agarithe.)* It has low salt-water tolerance, but high salt-wind tolerance.

If you are sick, this is your tree, as it is reputed to have medicinal effects for catarrh, edema, malaria, incontinence and venereal diseases. The tree comes from the Borage Family. The name, *Cordia* is after Valerius Cordus, a 16th Century German botanist. *Sebestena* refers to a Persian tree with similar seeds found near the town of Sebesta, in Iran. The tree has been useful for many millennium; Egyptian mummy cases were made out of the wood.

Plant this tree as a specimen in a prominent place in the yard or amongst other vegetation. It can be a street or a median strip tree or parking lot tree.

The tree sometimes looks trashy with leaves destroyed by the flashy, green Geiger beetle but the leaves grow right back. It can be a bit of a litterbug, but it is sure showy when grown in the midst of other vegetation. Other than the leaves the owner of this tree will have no serious pest problems.

The City of Key West has planted these trees on Rest Beach and Flagler Avenue. A specimen is at the Key West Garden Club.

Gumbo-limbo *(Bursera simaruba)*

Gumbo-limbo Tree Laughs at the Wind

During the Sculpture Key West installation in the Key West Garden Club after Hurricane Wilma in 2005, I noticed a stone marker indicating that there was a piece of artwork in the Butterfly Garden, but I did not see anything that I recognized as sculpture. It was only when I stood in the back of the garden that I suddenly saw the plethora of small black feathered birds created by the artist perched in the bare branches of a gumbo limbo (Borsora simaruba.)

The deciduous gumbo-limbo normally loses its leaves in spring, but this one had not had any leaves for the five months before the sculpture show. In fact, it did not have leaves for almost a year according to Rosi Ware, then president of the Garden Club. Gumbo-limbo trees can lose their leaves in a drought as well as a hurricane but eventually recover as they can make chlorophyll in their bark. This one was a survivor and is still gracing the butterfly garden.

That is the kind of native tree that we should clone, and it is easy enough to do, although some say that cloned trees are not as strong as trees grown from seeds unless they are pruned carefully. Cut a branch off of the tree; stick it in the ground and watch as a new tree emerges. In fact, you could take a twelve-inch trunk, bury it in the ground, and it will grow. In Costa Rica and throughout Central America people have used the trunks, placed closely together, to quickly grow a fence.

This common canopy tree can be frequently found planted along the streets and can grow

22

to 30 to 40 feet in height. Its common name comes from the Bantu language *nkombo* pertaining to a run-away slave and *edimbu* that means birdlime. The Calusa Indians used the sticky resin in the bark to trap songbirds.

Its large, open form makes it a great shade tree as wide as it is tall. The tree is easily recognized by its trunk's oily red skin that peels off to expose green bark. Key West locals call it the "tourist tree" because, like the tourist, it is often red and peeling. If it is scoured by hurricanes the trunk can become covered with a sensual gray patina. The gummy resin has been used to make glue, varnish, and liniment.

The alternate and pinnately compound leaves are shiny, bright green on the top and lighter on the bottom. Leaflets with pointed ends are two to three inches long, and there may be two to eight leaflets on a leaf. The gumbo-limbo trees are deciduous with leaves falling in the spring. They make great mulch. If the leaves are smashed, they smell like turpentine. Natives made a tea from the leaves for dysentery, fever and low blood pressure, but I don't recommend a tea that tastes like turpentine. The bark is a folk medicine antidote for poisonwood, poison ivy and bee and wasp stings.

Gumbo-limbo has panicles of inconspicuous, cream-colored flowers. Seeds are encapsulated in a quarter-inch, ball shaped, reddish-brown capsule. The tree is drought, wind and salt tolerant. It grows well in alkaline, sandy, well-drained soil. Trees in this torchwood family (Burseraceae) are used for incense and include the trees that produce frankincense and myrrh.

The soft spongy wood is easily carved and was used to make carousel horses before they were molded out of plastic. It has been used for matches, charcoal, crates, boxes and interior trim. In case you are compelled to make a canoe out of a tree trunk, the gumbo-limbo resin is handy for coating the outside of the canoe to keep it watertight. Haitians prize the wood for drums.

Wildlife loves the tree as its leaves provide larval food and its flowers provide nectar for the dingy purple-wing butterfly (Eunica monima.) Mockingbirds, flycatchers and vireos eat the attractive but mostly inedible one-fourth inch triangular seeds for the same reason that chickens eat pebbles, to grind up food in their crops.

The American Forests: National Register of Big Trees' website lists the largest gumbo-limbo as 178 inches in circumference, 43 feet in height, with a 63 foot spread. A large specimen tree is at St. Mary's Star of the Sea Church in Key West and another at the Key West Garden Club.

Inkwood (*Exothea paniculata)*

Inkwood Can Keep Your Love Life Growing

If you were caught in a rockland hammock and you desperately needed to write a love letter, you could seek out the inkwood sap which blackens when dry. Then write your epistle on a dried sea grape leaf. Or you could draw a map showing the rock under which lies the buried treasure. Think like a youngster playing in the woods and the native inkwood tree turns into an interesting tree indeed.

Inkwood *(Exothea paniciulata)* is a fairly common citizen of rockland hammocks in the Keys where it dwells among the limestone rocks that are often exposed near the surface of the land. Depending on the nutrients available to the trees, they usually grow from 25 to 35 feet in height with a circumference of 6 to 15 inches and are either a sub-canopy or a canopy tree. The American Forests: National Register of Big Trees' website lists the largest specimen, which is found in Monroe County, as 47 feet in height with a crown spread of 28 feet and a trunk circumference of 47 inches.

They have tall trunks with gray bark exposing reddish-brown under-bark. The bark is thin, mottled and separates into large scales. Interestingly, it is covered with pores that allow for more gas exchange. The sap turns black when exposed to the air, which may account for its name, inkwood.

The leaves are compound with two to four leaflets per leaf that are two to five inches long. They are dark green and shiny on top. They are evergreen and their edges are slightly wavy. According to *Native Florida Plants*, by Robert G. Haehle and Joan Brookwell, the leaves "grow at the ends of the branches." It has clusters of flowers in the spring that are white with an orange center. Male and female flowers are segregated on different plants. To add a little spice to their lives, occasionally, a few flowers of the opposite sex or bi-sexual flowers show up on the same plant. The one-half-inch fruit on the female trees begins as orange ball and turns deep purple when it ripens in the fall.

John Henderson, botanist at Crane Point Hammock, said that often the trees of the hammock continually flower and fruit at slightly different times, providing food for the birds on a consistent basis.

A rockland hammock is a rare community that occurs on a thin layer of highly organic soil in an area where the limestone is often exposed and the floor is covered with leaf litter. This area does not regularly flood. It is dependent on a high water table to nourish its plants. It hosts as many as 120 diverse species of trees and shrubs and other plants. Generally, the more mature trees are in the center while the margins are covered with a dense growth of shrubs.

Henderson described how difficult it was to identify the plants in a quadrant of the 63-acre Crane Point Hammock in Marathon because the foliage was too dense to penetrate. High winds and a lowered water table affect rockland hammocks. At Big Pine Key the underlying rock type changes from a porous Key Largo limestone to a less permeable oolitic limestone. So even though the upper and middle Keys receive more rainfall than the Big Pine Key rocklands, there is less standing water. As a result, according to Henderson, the trees and shrubs at Crane Point Hammock are shorter and scrawnier, forming Keys thickets. The lower elevation of Crane Point may also contribute to the smaller growth.

The swirling wood grains of the inkwood tree are highly prized by woodworkers for crafts. The wood is hard, heavy, durable and close-grained. In the past, it has been used for pilings and boat building because it is resistant to shipworms, a saltwater clam that burrows into wood.

Jamaica Caper (*Capparis cynophallophora*)

Fecund Jamaica Caper Relies on Perfect Flowers

The Jamaica caper (*Capparis cynophallophora*) is a widely popular large shrub or tree that emits a nightly fragrance that will stop a sensitive human in a heartbeat. The three-inch, brush-like flowers start out white and blush to a deep maroon within a few hours. A white, four-petaled flower forms the base. It is called perfect in the botanical world because male and female parts are found on the same flower. Alec Bristow in *The Sex Life of Plants* states that plants invented sex long before the first animals appeared, and when plants invented sex, they also invented beauty.

This hermaphrodite-like flower in the Capparaceae Family has an unusual anatomy. Remember your high school botany? The caper's orange-tipped female pistil is shorter than the male stamens that have the pollen grains. The pollen-filled anthers on purple stamens droop dejectedly far beneath the tubes they need to enter. How does the pollen reach the end of the pistil tube? The showy flowers start blooming in April and attract a myriad of insects, bees, and butterflies, and lizards. Even the wind gets to flirt with moving that pollen. Somehow, with their help, the caper gets pregnant. Flowers get pollinated and produce viable seeds.

Immediately after pollination, the male anthers wilt. The seedpods begin to form in the rainy season and grow to a length of six-inches. These truly amazing seedpods burst open and contain brilliant orange-red, sticky pulp around the seeds. It is Christmas in September for the birds, with the red seedpods dangling from the branches like ornaments. I observed two doves and a rare white-crowned pigeon precariously balanced on the thin branches, contorting their bodies to reach the pulpy plunder. The messy birds get it all over their feathers. Ants devour pulp that drops on the ground. (The Jamaica caper flower-bud is related to the edible caper served in salads, but it is not edible.)

Delicate, pastel-bronze leaves are folded together when they emerge. As they mature, these three-inch, evergreen leaves turn dark, shiny green on the top and a shimmering silver color underneath. You can identify the oval leaf because it has a little dimple at the tip. The dense leaves rustle, softly singing in the breeze.

Thin branches encourage its use by small wildlife. Dense foliage turns the Jamaica caper into an excellent barrier to hide an unpleasant view or create privacy. It is sturdy and can take being planted along highways. It would be lovely in a spot that gets foot traffic in the evening to take advantage of the fragrance of its flowers. It can be pruned into a tree by cutting off the lower branches or be cut as a hedge.

Its showy flowers and seeds turn this shrub into a specimen plant for the yard. The 12-foot native survived Hurricane Wilma as a front line tree on our beach. It was inundated by salt-water flooding and direct winds and survived. It grows with poor nutrition in our alkaline, sandy soil. Seedlings pop up under the branches and transplant well. Direct sun will produce the fastest growth. For a less dense, open look, put it in the shade.

No serious pests or diseases attack this Keys native. Planting scarified seeds will result in propagation. Often there are seedlings under the branches of the trees that can be transplanted. It is readily available in nurseries.

An example of the Jamaica Caper can be seen at the Key West Garden Club.

Jamaica Dogwood (*Piscidia piscipula*)

The Fishfuddle Fostered Fast Fishing

In May, the native Jamaica dogwood tree *(Piscidia piscipula)* loses all of its leaves. Tiny pink flowers that look like minuscule hummingbirds form all over the ends of its branches. They are so sweet with nectar that the bees, wasps and insects are compelled to its blooms by the thousands. The entire tree looks as though it's quivering in the sunlight.

I live on the fourth floor above a 40-foot specimen of the tree and look down on this quivering mass of insects in the orgiastic sating of their hunger. It's like the insects found a tree of Godiva chocolate.

As sweet as the nectar of this tree is, when its leaves, bark and branches are ground into a powder and thrown into the water, they create a poison that stuns the nervous system of cold-blooded fish. The Seminoles threw the mixture into the water in order to pick the fish off the top of the water instead of catching them. Not very sporting, but effective when a tribe needs feeding.

Evidently, this paralytic effect doesn't occur when it is used with warm-blooded animals as the roots, twigs and bark have been used as a sedative to reduce muscle spasms, induce sleep, relieve pain and reduce inflammation. The roots and bark have been used as a powerful narcotic similar to morphine. Its fruits make poison for arrows.

The active ingredient is the chemical rotenone used in pesticides, insecticides and piscicides. The piscicides are used by fish nurseries to cull out unwanted exotics. This chemical is poorly absorbed by humans.

The intensity of the chemical differs when trees are grown in different kinds of soils just as food grown on organic soil differs from food grown in land that has been depleted. Although long used in traditional medicines, these medicinal effects are word of mouth, as they haven't been studied by western medicine so I don't advise trying them out.

The scientific name of this fast-growing tree means little-fish killer. Jamaica dogwood is variously called Florida fishpoison tree or better yet, fishfuddle. Even more interesting, the dogwood portion of the name comes from the boomerang shaped piece of bent wood that is used on a ship's bow where the mermaid usually hangs out on the prow. It was made from this tree's strong, decay-resistant wood. It's good for building boats and fence posts. It grows so well that sometimes the fence posts get roots.

Jamaica dogwood's semi-deciduous leaves are alternate and pinnately compound. Three-inch leaflets form in an opposite arrangement with as many as ten on a stem. They are medium green above and lighter underneath.

Seeds are light brown with four papery wings holding red-brown seeds that flutter down in August. This member of the Fabaceae Family germinates readily in eight to ten days. Our well-drained, nutrient-poor soils suit the Jamaica dogwood well. The fast-growing dogwood is moderately tolerant of salt-winds, drought, and short-term inundation by salt water.

It is an ornamental tree in tropical hammocks where it rises above the under-story trees and enjoys the full sun that its height provides. Hundreds of them grow along Highway 1 between Key West and Islamorada. It does not like cold weather and exists primarily in Zone 11. It is the larval host plant for several butterfly species including: the native cassius blue butterfly (*Leptots cassius*) and hammock skipper (*Polygonus leo.*)

Joewood (*Jacquinia keynensis*)

Threatened Joewood Easily Grown from Seed

Pity the snowbirds who do not get to see joewood *(Jacquinia keynensis)* in its full reproductive power.

This hurricane-resistant, ten-foot tree grows near the coast and survives salt-wind without a whimper. It can take moderate salt-water inundation and has moderate drought tolerance. Sandy or limestone soils provide enough nutrients. Growing in coastal hammocks, barrier islands and coastal thickets, its small, thick, stiff, ovate leaves create an excellent wind barrier. It is considered threatened by the State of Florida.

It is about as broad as it is tall and grows slowly. Its compact round-topped crown grows from a stout, short trunk. The trunk can get to be ten inches in diameter. Tiny white blossoms with yellow centers grace its branches. They are fragrant, but when touched, they feel like wax copies of flowers. The birds love its seeds. I have laughingly observed two doves struggling to land on its tight branches, flipping upside down in order to get at its bright red seeds. In the winter, these red seeds make the small tree look like the Keys version of a Christmas tree.

It is threatened for the same reasons as are other coastal hammock plants. So much destruction of environment has occurred due to clearing and building on the coasts that no room is left for the native plants that once used it as their habitat. Species, such as native joewood, are closely tied to wildlife and when one plant is threatened it also endangers others, affecting the species that rely on the threatened plant for food or shelter.

This plant can be grown from seed fairly easily. Remove the seed from the berry and plant it just under the surface. Do not wait for the seed to dry out before planting it, as the seed doesn't sprout well if it gets old. Often seedlings sprout under the tree and can be easily transplanted. There is another joewood native to the Bahamas (*Jacquinia arborea* or braceletwood.) The Bahama joewood has bigger and more succulent leaves in a lighter color green. It has become more prevalent in the Keys and should not be planted in the landscape as it is beginning to be invasive.

Cudjoe Key was possibly named for the joewood as the tree is also called cudjoewood. Historian John Viele of Summerland Key believes that Cudjoe, which was a common West African name, was the name of a fugitive slave or free Negro who lived on the island at some point prior to Gerdes' Coast Guard survey in 1849.

A native joewood can be found in the native gardens at the Key West Garden Club and a larger one in the McCoy Indigenous Park in Key West.

Lignum vitae (Guaiacum sanctum)

Key West Garden Club Gives Tree of Life - A New Life

The beautiful tree of life (*Lignum vitae/Guaiacum sanctum*) is considered endangered by the State of Florida and critically imperiled by the Florida Institute for Regional Conservation. That is why the Key West Garden Club has begun The *Lignum Vitae* Tree of Life Conservation Project that endeavors to propagate and introduce more of these trees in the Keys.

In myth, the wood of the *Lignum vitae* was found in the Garden of Eden and was used for the Holy Grail; therefore, it was called holy wood. Whoever consumed its resin was given perpetual health, immortality, and protection from weakness and infirmity. A pulverized potion of its wood was thought to be an aphrodisiac. Merlin's staff was reputedly made of the wood, as was the bathtub in Gabriel Garcia Marquez's book *Love in the Time of Cholera.*

The Native Americans taught the Spanish how to extract its resin to make purges, cathartics and antiseptics, treating arthritis, asthma, diabetes, high blood pressure, gout, malaria, rheumatism, syphilis and TB. It was considered the penicillin of its day. It was thought to neutralize poisons and serve as a contraceptive. It is still used in modern medicine as a test for hidden blood.

Christopher Columbus originally brought it to Europe and declared, "It is immune to all destructive organisms." By 1500 its wood was regularly shipped from the Keys to Europe. Later, timber cutters from the Bahamas decimated large tracts of *Lignum vitae* forests making the wood into dishes, mallets, bowling balls, butcher blocks, guitar picks and Billy clubs.

Shipbuilders desired it because it was extremely hard and dense. The Navy used it in WW II to make the submarine propeller-shaft bearings for the USS Pampanito. The hinges and locks made from the wood lasted over 100 years in the Erie Canal. It was called *el palo para muchas cosas*, the wood of many uses, and that was its downfall. The wood may have been long lasting, but the stock of living trees never recovered.

Many of the trees were destroyed from 1850 to 1900 when Keys land was cleared for agricultural plantations. Russ and Charlotte Niedhauk, caretakers of Lignumvitae Key for many years, helped facilitate the purchase of the island by the state. Lignumvitae Key Botanical State Park (MM 78.5) was declared a protected historic site in 1971. However, the tree is still endangered and exists in the U.S. mainly in the Keys.

The compound leaf is comprised of six to ten bright green, one-inch leaflets per leaf. Because its wood is thirty percent resin, it is self-lubricating. Once sanded, the surface of the wood looks like it has been varnished. One cubic foot of its trunk weighs 82 pounds and the tree, whose specific gravity is 1.39, sinks when immersed in water. The tree trunk is short and gnarled and the tree is as broad as it is tall.

Clusters of unusual three-fourth-inch bright-blue, five-petaled flowers attract bees and butterflies, especially the obligate Kricogonia lysid (sulphur lysid) as the tree is its only larval food. Red fruit covers a black seed that lies in an orange five-part seedpod that pops open and ejects its seeds throughout the year. Both catbirds and mockingbirds find the seeds a tasty treat.

Lignum vitae trees like full or partial sun and well-drained but moist soil. It survives salt-water inundation and salt wind, but it cannot handle long periods of salt-water intrusion. With patience, it's easy to grow from the seedlings sprouting under the trees. The Key West Garden Club has taken a special interest in growing this endangered tree. They are slow growing but do better with regular fertilizer. They also bonsai well.

The native *Lignum vitae* grows to a height of 37 feet with trunks two feet in diameter. Its bark is pale gray and rough. Its growth rings are not distinct so it is difficult to determine a tree's age. A full-grown example is just to the left of the entrance to the gardens of the Key West Garden Club. There are six species in the Zygopyllaceae Family and the larger leaved Cuban version is in a fenced section of the Key West cemetery (with the little deer.) This *Lignum vitae* has a trunk over four feet in circumference.

Special thanks to Denise Knerr who created a comprehensive brochure about the *Lignum vitae* tree for the Key West Garden Club in 1996 and Janice Duquesnel for her botanical expertis

West Indian Mahogany *(Swietenia mahagoni)*

Threatened Mahogany Is "Unobtanium" Wood

West Indian mahogany (Swietenia mahagoni) is native to the middle and upper Keys, but according to some authorities, not as far south as Key West. Still, these giants grace our city streets creating cool shade on the hot pavement.

Regrettably, some were planted without thinking of the electrical lines above them. The electric power utility has been forced to cut huge V's in the center of the trees because they interfere with power lines. This practice results in seriously weakened trees. Locally, we call these Y-shaped trees "the silly mahoganies."

These 50-foot trees have an erect trunk and a broad, dense crown sometimes as wide as it is tall. The brownish bark is thick and rough. Semi-deciduous leaves fall in the springtime. Mayan farmers timed their spring corn planting with the advent of inconspicuous but highly fragrant flowers on the mahogany. The four to eight inch, evenly pinnate, compound leaves of the mahogany are a luscious dark-green.

The West Indian mahogany tree was widely prized for making furniture, flooring, boats and musical instruments such as guitars, drums and pianos. Heavy lumbering caused it to become threatened in the State of Florida. Now, most of the 15 related species of the mahogany used in the world is farmed in the Philippines, Africa, Malaysia, and China.

Mahogany was planted in Key West by early settlers and according to the criteria of defining a native plant according to method of dispersal, is not native to the ecosystem of Key

West. Native plants arrive here by natural means. If humans brought the plant to the area, it is not considered native. The mahogany tree is native only to the islands closer to the mainland beginning around Upper Matecumbe Key.

According to *The Florida Keys: A History of the Pioneers* by John Viele the last Indian natives were taken to Cuba in 1793 and for 56 years the Keys was either British or Spanish without either country being in control. Cuba called the islands "Norte de Habana" and issued fishing licenses for the waters. Bahamian vessels plundered wood.

The British governor was told to put a stop to the intrusions but had no means to do so. In the mean time, when the Spanish controlled the islands, the Bahamians went about their pillaging of what Viele called "mahogany and other valuable hard wood. "He goes on to say," By 1769, most of the valuable timber on the Keys had been cut down."

In *The Commodore's Story*, by Ralph Middleton Munroe and Vincent Gilpin, re-published by the Historical Association of Southern Florida in 1966 from the original published in 1930, "Mr. Holden had been especially attracted by the mahogany of the keys, locally called madeira. It is the true *Sweetenia* (sic) *mahogany*, but the timber is much darker, harder, redder and more elaborately grained than the usual Honduras wood, owing to the fact that it grows very slowly on the barren rock ridges of the Keys."

The elder Mr. Holden agreed to identify mahogany trees in the rockland hammocks from Key Largo to Upper Matecumbe Key for the South Florida Lumber Company owned by his son John Holden and William Barrows, a Mystic shipbuilder. What Holden found in 1890 was an impenetrable jungle with scattered timber. "The average diameter being eleven inches with very few as high as three feet (sic); while in the low forest the trunks were not high nor particularly straight." The company cut the timber and piled it on the shoreline to be picked up later by a three-masted schooner.

When the schooner arrived in New York, the wood was criticized for the color variation from standard mahogany and for its small size and dark streaks. Eventually, it was sold for hammer handles and sewing machine cases. Now wood that is harder and elaborately grained is known in guitar-making circles as "unobtanium " because it is so difficult to find.

The wood is a yellowish-pink color when it is first cut and turns deep red as it ages. The tree is a native so it is drought and salt-wind tolerant and likes well-drained, poor-nutrient soils.

While the flowers of the West Indian mahogany tree may be nothing to speak of, the seedpods are spectacular. Pale green, baseball-sized seedpods form on the tree and ripen there until they become a warm brown. Then they pop open scattering winged seeds everywhere and dropping their thick, wood-like seed pod casings on the ground around the tree. It's a messy tree.

Milkbark - *Drypetes diversifolia*

Standout White Bark Draped Around an Erect Trunk

Imagine that the endangered white milkbark tree *(Drypetes diversifolia)* is dressed in pure white silk seductively draped around the erect trunk. She is an impressive citizen of a rockland hammock. Stand back and watch her among the dark grays and browns of other hammock partygoers and realize that there are few of these beauties around.

There are more than 400 plants identified as endangered by the state and over a 100 that are listed as threatened. The Keys are a delicate ecosystem that can be disrupted by falling water tables, high winds, and flooding. Habitat destruction and habitat fragmentation account for most designations of threatened or endangered status. Trees, like the milkbark, that have a tenuous hold in the environment, are always at risk.

Jewels pinned to her frock accessorize this hammock beauty. They are gray, brown and yellow lichens, a combination of an algae and a fungus. If a tree is planted outside of the microhabitat of the hammock, these lichens will most likely not form because the environmental conditions will not be the same so the beauty of the milkbark in the woods may not translate to a backyard environment. The tree is a feeding ground for the even more rare Stock Island tree snail that frequents the hammock understories.

The height of the tree depends on the ground in which it grows, but generally milkbark is 20 to 30 feet in height and likes moist, but well-drained soils. It grows vertically, taller than it is broad in light shade. There is no American Forests: National Register of Big Trees' web listing for this species, but the one in the Key West Tropical Forest and Botanical Gardens is over 40-feet tall.

It is moderately drought tolerant and does not thrive with flooding or salt-winds.

These pure flower children in white were probably sent to boarding schools as their blooms are dioecious, that is girl and boy flowers are on separate plants. The inconspicuous yellowish-white flowers bloom all year in clusters or individually at the leaf axil. Flowering peaks in the summer.

The quarter-inch fruit is oval and white. It has a single seed inside its somewhat dry pulp. *Drypetes*, the scientific name, is a Greek word for drupe, which describes the fruit.

Mature leaves are alternate, stiff, oval and dark-green above. They measure two to three inches long and one and one half inches-wide. The margins of the young leaves often have spines like feisty teenagers. The spines may be a defense against predators who might like to nibble on the tender new growth. Older leaves have entire margins and are smooth-edged. The *diverisfolia* in its scientific name refers to the different shapes of the young and mature leaves of this semi-deciduous tree. Sprouts grow from roots around the tree.

The wood in the milkbark is not affected by wood-boring shipworms and so it often was used by early settlers as dock pilings.

Milkbark is the larval host plant for the Florida white butterfly *(Appias drusilla.)* Picture the white bark of this beauty with white butterflies flitting around it and snap that mind-picture to bring back whenever you think of the unusual charm of milkbark.

This tree can be seen at the Key West Botanical Gardens and at Fort Zachary Taylor.

Myrsine, colicwood *(Rapanea punctata)*

Mild Mannered Myrsine Thrives Almost Anywhere

There are over 1,000 species in the Myrsinaceae Family, but only two of them are in Florida, myrsine *(Rapanea punctata)* and marlberry *(Ardisia escalloniodes.)* Mild-mannered myrsine is a small understory tree that is widely cultivated because it is so versatile. It politely grows almost anywhere it is planted, but it is often found on the backsides of coastal dunes. It is more prevalent in the Lower Keys than the Upper Keys.

Moderate growing, the 15-foot tree has an erect trunk usually two to three inches in diameter, and a narrow crown. It grows more vertical than horizontal.

Thick, leathery, dark-green leaves are oblong, blunt-ended, two to five inches long and about two inches wide. Their shiny surfaces curve under on the margins and cluster on the ends of branches creating room for the flowers and berries under them. Leaves are arranged in an alternate pattern.

The one-eigth-inch flowers are white with thin purple stripes and cluster on the previous year's stem growth. They are dioecious with male and female flowers on different plants. They look quite similar to the flower on the willow bustic tree. The flowers are sessile, which means lacking a stem. They grow directly on the twigs. Peak flowering occurs in the fall-winter seasons.

Jays, woodpeckers, cardinals, and catbirds go crazy for the small ripe, dark-blue berry. The sessile berries are clustered on the new grown stems in leaf axils. There is one seed inside each berry. Berries ripen one by one, providing wildlife food for months.

Myrsine can be grown in a wide variety of well-drained soils, but thrives with some organic material. It can tolerate short periods of drought and has a high tolerance to salt wind. It cannot survive long-term flooding. Either full sun or part shade is acceptable to the agreeable myrsine.

The scientific name, *Rapanea* was Latinized from an aboriginal Indian vernacular name. *Punctata* means spotted and refers to small glands that look like puncture wounds on the leaves. Miccosukee Indians dried the leaves and added them to extend and flavor tobacco. They called the tree white tobacco-seasoning tree. Although the thin gray bark was used for tanning, the tree has no present commercial or medicinal value. Myrsine is susceptible to scale.

The versatility of this tree makes it desirable to plant. It grows well in many different environments and will attract a plethora of birds to a yard. Use it for natural screening or as a specimen plant. Since its growth is vertical, it's a good choice for narrow spaces.

Oysterwood *(Gymnanthes lucida)*

Oysterwood - Dense and Colorful and Prized

The beautiful, hard wood of the native oysterwood tree is highly desired by woodworkers. Its sapwood is yellow and its heartwood is a dark reddish-brown. When hurricanes come through the Keys and trees are broken or uprooted, woodworkers re-create a dry land version of the old Key West salvagers. They go tree hunting. Oysterwood survives hurricanes so there is little of it to find.

Mark Butler, who owns a small sawmill business, called Urban Forest Recyclers, in Tavernier, FL, says, "Urban Forest Recycling salvages unusual Caribbean-basin hardwoods. Because of the semi-tropical climate and unusual growing conditions of the Keys, the wood from these trees--all non-commercial species--is generally denser and more colorful than that of typical trees of these species."

Buffed oysterwood takes on a sheen that looks like an oyster shell, hence the name. It is made into carvings, belt buckles, jewelry, turnings, bowls, musical instruments, poles, posts, walking sticks and handles.

Oysterwood is an erect, evergreen, semi-deciduous small tree growing in hardwood hammocks most usually to 15 feet in height. It is usually taller than it is broad. According to the American Forests: National Register of Big Trees' website the largest tree is in Monroe County and is 30 feet tall with a 13 feet spread and 17 inch circumference. Even when it is big, it is not very big.

It likes full or partial sunshine and can withstand drought once established and it does not succumb to cold weather. It resides deep in the hammock so it is protected from direct salt spray. It has a low tolerance to salt water. It can be pruned into a one-stemmed tree or left with multi-stemmed bushier trunks.

Its dark-green leaves are alternate, leathery and elliptical, Two to four inches long and one inch wide. New growth is a lush rose color. The leaves are tough textured with pronounced veins on the surface.

There are both male and female flowers on the same plant. The tiny, one-quarter-inch greenish-yellow male catkins are arranged on three two-inch spikes at the terminus of a branch. Pink female flowers occur individually on separate stalks that are wind pollinated. Some homosexual plants have only male flowers and will not produce fruit.

Oysterwood is the larval host plant for the Florida purplewing butterfly (*Eunica tatila.*) These butterflies look brown with white spots, but flip their purple sheens when photographed with a flash camera. They pose at odd angles on the trunks and under leaves.

The trunks are gray and peeling to show the reddish-brown underbark. Oysterwood tree fruit is small, subglobose, (that means kind of round) and has three lobes that make it look like a tiny pumpkin. It is carried individually on short stems and turns dark black when ripe. Many native birds eat it.

The tree can be used as a tall hedge or as a specimen plant and can provide an air-conditioner shade between houses. Oysterwood, also called crabwood, can be found, labeled, at the McCoy Indigenous Park near the turtle pond and at the Key West Botanical Gardens on Stock Island.

Paradise Tree *(Simarouba glauca)*

Native Paradise Tree More Useful Than Google

The paradise tree is a marvelous creation. As all green plants do, it mops up carbon dioxide and produces oxygen. Its leaves provide shade and then fall to the ground as life giving mulch. Its roots prevent soil erosion. One acre of trees can eat 500 kg of carbon dioxide in a year. It grows in wastelands where other farm products won't grow, doesn't need water, is easily propagated from seeds or cuttings and is a cash crop. It is believed to be named paradise tree because it can only live in a frost-free environment, such as our Paradise, the Florida Keys.

This tree's seed produces edible oil that is used in baking in Central America and India. It is often called oil tree or bitterwood. The oil does not contain bad cholesterol. The oilseed cake (what's left after the oil is squeezed out) is full of nitrogen, phosphorus and potash and makes a good fertilizer. Its shells can be used to make particleboard and the termite-resistant wood can be used to make furniture, toys, matches and paper. The fruit pulp is sweet and is used to make beverages when the birds don't eat it.

Every part of the tree is used for medicinal purposes. Natives use it to cure intestinal parasites, fevers, malaria, diarrhea, dysentery, anemia, colitis, herpes, influenza, polio, West Nile virus and other viruses, stomach and bowel disorders, as an astringent for wounds and sores, to stop bleeding and as a tonic. It is currently being studied as a toxin to cancer and leukemia cells. Quite a list! It is purported to cure everything from a tummy ache to cancer. If that is not enough, it is also used as a skin toner. It improves hydration, helping to retain moisture and will get rid of liver spots. This tree is more useful than Google.

The miracle substances found in the paradise tree are quassinoids. Scientists have known about several of the four-syllable substances found in the quassinoids, for years. Currently, a number of experiments are being done with them.

In parts of the world where the sustainability of farming is in question because of global warming and related droughts, this member of the Simaroubaceae Family can be planted and six years later, the first crop of fruit can be harvested. The wasteland can sustain a dense crop of trees and will gradually improve the soil. It can live to be a seventy-year-old granddad. Termites don't attack it, cattle, goats and sheep do not eat it, and it has virtually no pests. It's a safe bet that deer also do not like it. Economically viable and ecologically sustainable, this is a tree for the twenty-first century.

The paradise tree is native to Key West and has low salt water tolerance, but high drought and salt wind tolerance, although it loses branches easily in the wind. Alkaline soil is its caviar. Towering above the tropical Florida hammocks forty feet high is its large round crown enjoying full sun. Thick, rough, dark gray bark covers its trunk and branches. Its tiny yellow flowers occur on female and male trees. The females produce more fruit than males and so agronomists around the world are trying to graft the most productive trees to increase the output of the oil in third world countries.

The bright red drupes turn black when they get ripe and can be a bit of a litter problem; if they are planted by the roadsides they will stain sidewalks, but birds love them. A second problem with this tree is that its roots remain near the surface and can push up sidewalks and roads.

Compound leaves with 10 to 12 leaflets per leaf emerge as a creamy, copper-red, like dusting the tree with paprika before they turn green. If you plant one now it is so fast growing that it will be big before your kids are. Propagation is from a seed that germinates quickly and grows rapidly. You can see this tree at the Key West Garden Club in the native garden.

The western world is busy discovering the many uses of the aptly named paradise tree.

Pigeon Plum *(Coccoloba diversifolia)*

Pigeon Plum – A Shady Character

The native pigeon plum tree (*Coccoloba diversifolia*) is a close cousin of the seagrape (*Coccoloba uvifera*) and is a member of the buckwheat family, Polygonaceae. Cocco means that the fruit "contains one seed." Diversifolia means "diverse foliage" due to its variously shaped and sized leaves when it is young.

This tree is a mensch, a real man. He doesn't show off with flashy flowers or spectacular seeds. He simply does his job in the tropical hammock with grace and order.

The evergreen leaves are sometimes two to four inches long and other times four to eight inches long hence the name diversifolia, which means diverse foliage. They are thick and generally oval-shaped. They occur as simple leaves in an alternate configuration on the branches. The shiny, dark-green leaves are densely packed on the tree making a compact shape, up to 40 feet in height and 20 feet in width. The leaves fall in early spring, but re-grow immediately with red-tinged leaf sprouts until chlorophyll forms in the leaves.

The trunk of the tree, which resembles the sea grape's trunk, often has embedded or included bark formations. These do not weaken the stalwart tree. When the tree is mature, mottled gray bark peels away to a rust-colored under-bark. Beautiful patterns emerge. I'm reminded of a subtle fabric for a man's suit jacket that is lined in rust-colored silk, not ostentatious, but classy.

This native tree is strong and break resistant. It can be planted back from the salt spray but tolerates salty soil if it is well drained; a perfect tree for our alkaline nutrient-poor soil. It will thrive in full sun or partial shade. It has low salt-water tolerance and moderate salt wind tolerance.

The wildly fragrant, small, white flowers grow on three-inch bracts and turn into a dark-purple fruit beloved by birds. These fruits are edible raw, dried or made into jelly or wine. They were an important food of the Miccosukee Indians. Blooms occur over the summer.

This forest gentleman is happy to provide superb shelter for birds, food for bees and butterflies and even a scratching post for raccoons. It attracts the rare Schaus' swallowtail butterfly (*Heraclides aristodemus*), the orange sulphur (*Poebis agarithe*), warblers, vireos, and the endangered white-crowned pigeons.

Inconspicuous, one-third-inch-long, purple fruit frequently appear mid-summer. The tree continues to flower and fruit year-round. Although I have spoken about this tree as a gentleman, there are both male and female trees. Only the female tree bears fruit.

Weevils may attack trees that are stressed. One common method to get rid of the weevils is to spray the tree with a powerful hose and knock them to the ground and their subsequent death. Even if the weevils destroy the leaves, the tree will come back. The tree can be propagated from seed. Its growth rate is moderate.

The lovely pigeon plum can be planted on streets, in parking lots, in native gardens, as a shade tree, near a deck or patio, a median strip, as buffer plantings, formal hedges or as a specimen tree. Its canopy will provide shade. The State of Florida highly recommends this tree and suggests that it be planted more often. The National Champion pigeon plum tree can be found at the back of the pond in the Key West Tropical Forests and Botanical Gardens on Stock Island. A specimen is at the Key West Garden Club.

This stately gentleman could elegantly grace any lawn in South Florida.

Poisonwood Tree (*Metopium toxiferum*)

Poisonwood – Friendly to Everything, Except People

Not all plants are nice to people. The aptly named poisonwood tree (*Metopium toxiferum*) is beautiful and important to wildlife but dangerous to some humans! Poison ivy, Brazillian pepper, sumac and cashews are its cousins in the Anacardiaceae Family. However, not everyone who is allergic to the tree's sap is allergic to the pollen.

Why do we want this tree? It may make us break out but it is a cornucopia of treasures for native wildlife. Its nectar feeds butterflies such as the Bahamian swallowtail *(Papilio andracmon,)* Florida white *(Appias Drusilla,)* giant swallowtail *(Papilio cresphontes,)* Julia *(Dryas iulia,)* large orange sulphur *(Colias eurytheme,)* mangrove skipper *(Phocides pigmalion,)* southern broken-dash *(Wallengrenia otho)* and many others.

The especially beautiful poisonwood is a native plant that you should recognize and avoid, but it is an essential part of rockland hammocks and its presence supports myriad forms of life. The tree grows to 25 feet in height and is taller than it is wide, but it also can be a ten-foot bush. Other than in the Keys, it also grows in the Caribbean, Central America, the West Indies and Everglades National Park. It thrives in our well-drained, nutrient-poor soil. Often it grows in a tropical hammock as a pioneer under-story tree beneath taller trees.

The glossy leaves vary from four to ten inches long. They are dark-green with a yellow mid-rib and yellow along the margins. They are compound with typically five to seven ovate leaflets per leaf including the terminal leaflet. The leaflets are three inches long and two inches wide. Sometimes you can see black sap spotting the leaflets as a result of insects probing into the leaflets to obtain nutrients. Poisonwood drops its leaves and replaces them in the early spring. Panicles of small greenish-white flowers with five petals occur in the spring.

The one-eighth-inch orange fruit feeds raccoons and the skittish and endangered white-crowned pigeons *(Patagioenas leucocephala.)* The fruits are high in lipids that the young white-crowned pigeons rely on to increase their fat content while in the nest. There is a direct correlation between years of high productivity of poisonwood fruit to successful fledging of white-crowned pigeons.

The reddish-brown bark flakes off into large plates and if damaged, clear sap oozes out and quickly turns black. If you touch the sap, even if you wash it off with soap and water, you may start to itch and then red pustules will open up. If you touch them, you may spread the rash all over your body. The itchy, burning blisters emerge as long as four days after contact with the tree. They are painful and can cause second-degree burns. The sap runs down the branches and into the stems and leaf veins. Simply brushing against a broken leaf may inflame you. Don't stand under poisonwood when it rains because its potent sap may drip on you. Although it won't jump out and attack, if it is burned its smoke and pollen can travel in the air and fill lungs with its sometimes-potent allergen or poison.

The initial contact area should be washed with WD-40 (Yes, the spray lubricant.) Soap and water don't work because the sap is not water-soluble. One of two folk remedies is to wipe the area of skin with gumbo-limbo bark *(Bursera simaruba)*, which is often found growing nearby in the tropical hammock. The second folk remedy is wiping the area with the juice of sour oranges. The rash was reported to be phototoxic so try to keep it out of the sun. Modern botanists recommend washing with Tecnu instead of trying old remedies.

Metopium refers to the sap of the tree and *toxiferum* to its toxicity.

Poisonwood can be seen in the newly planted Fran Ford White-crowned Pigeon Preserve on Government Road in Key West. It can be safely planted in this parkland area that is distant from frequent human traffic. There is one to the left of the entrance. Walk towards the end of the new trail and there are five more newly planted to provide food for the pigeons. They are also near the parking lot on the Fort View Trail in Ft. Zachary Taylor State Park.

Appreciate the wonders of poisonwood from the path. Don't touch the tree.

Red Mangrove *(Rhizophora mangle)*

Red Mangroves Protect the Shores

We could nickname the red mangrove *(Rhizophora mangle)* Martin diminutive of Mars. Like the god of war red mangrove is the protector of the shore. It provides hiding places and food for wildlife, crustaceans and young fish. It is a nursery for most marine organisms, which is why it is in turn a great feeding ground for wading birds. Its roots provide shelter for up to 90% of young Key fish. Yellow-crowned night herons, pelicans, white herons, ibis and frigatebirds nest and roost amongst its branches. Oysters, sponges, sea stars and *Cassiopeia* jellyfish also populate its habitat.

It cleans nitrates and chemical contaminants from the water. It creates and preserves land that might be washed away in storms. It protects and stabilizes shorelines from the destructiveness of wind and wave action. That is why mangrove preservation is of critical concern in the State of Florida. Red mangroves are critical to a healthy shoreline ecosystem as well as to the health of sea grass beds and coral reefs offshore.

There are three trees named mangrove, red, white and black, and they are not related to each other at all. What they do have in common is the ability to germinate seedlings on the parent tree. The mangrove group is ecological, not taxonomical.

Red mangrove is the most common in the 469,000 acres of mangrove in Florida. It is easily identified by its red prop roots that arch out into the mucky water. They create tannic acid and so the water is usually red around the roots. Roots were once used as ropes.

Its leaves are evergreen, dark on top and lighter on the bottom and vary from two to six inches long. They are ovate-shaped and covered with a waxy cuticle to prevent evaporation. Red mangroves want to retain as much moisture in their leaves as possible.

The tiny yellow flowers, which appear throughout the year, are generally wind-pollinated, but visited by insects and bees as well.

The two-inch cigar-shaped propagule contains a seed that germinates while still on the branches of the tree. After a year or more of development on the tree, the ten-inch propagule that contains the seed breaks away. It floats horizontally until the bottom section fills with water making it heavier. It turns upright so that when it encounters land it can embed itself in the sediment. This propagule can survive, floating vertically in the ocean, for over a year.

The dense growth of the mangrove is said to discourage human disturbance. E.O. Wilson said, "The only people who go into mangrove swamps are scientists and escaped convicts."

Scientists have discovered the process by which red mangroves obtain water and disperse salt. The arching aerial prop roots pull in magnesium from the air through tiny glands encased in warty nodules in the prop root.

Magnesium is a positive ion that forces other positive ions, like sodium, out of the root. This highly ionized state allows the plant to obtain water through reverse osmosis. The tides provide the wet-dry pattern. If salt does enter the plant, it is directed to several leaves that soon turn yellow and fall off.

Trimming red mangroves requires a permit and a certified arborist because of the nature of its growth. Red mangroves have growth buds only for the last three years of its growth. Therefore, if a tree is cut back too far, it will be unable to sprout new growth and it will die. Because of the incredibly important function of the mangrove ecosystem, it is important to understand the potential adverse impacts of trimming.

Red mangrove is the larval host for the mangrove skipper butterfly *(Phocides pigmalion)* and the io moth *(Automeris io)* and nectar plant for the mangrove skipper.

Red mangrove can be seen on North Roosevelt Boulevard, right before the Yacht Club doing its job as a protector of the sea wall. It also can be seen creating land in the estuary at the end of Riviera Canal in Key West.

Satinleaf Tree *(Chrysophyllum oliviforme)*

Flashy Satinleaf Shimmers in the Wind

The satinleaf tree (*Chrysophyllum oliviforme*) is a fun-loving flasher flipping her leaves in the breeze and displaying a dense, hair-covered, under-surface that is a luscious copper color. Like a go-go dancer she shimmers, vacillating between the shiny, deep green of her upper surface and the warm copper of her lower. Ovate-shaped leaves are four inches long and three-fourths-inch wide.

The native tree produces inconspicuous yellowish-green flowers from June to November. They sit next to the leaf on auxiliary clusters on the reddish-brown stems. Petals have five lobes and form a tiny bell shape. Insects pollinate them. Honeybees are particularly fond of the nectar.

The quarter-inch fruit is dark purple. Gummy white skin secretes a white sap when it is cut. The sweet seeds are edible and the skins can be chewed like gum. Birds go crazy for its feast of fruit and spread the seeds in wild abandon.

Satinleaf is in the Sapotaceae Family as is the non-native sapodilla from which chicle (used in gum) is obtained. Another Caribbean cousin is *caimito* that has a four-inch edible fruit. The name *Chrysophyllum* means golden leaf.

This evergreen tree grows to a height of 30 feet and never loses its leaves since new leaves grow as old leaves fall off. Satinleaf produces multiple stems. Cautious pruning is necessary to create a stronger one-trunked tree. Drooping branches may also be pruned. The trunk is slender and covered in reddish-brown bark. If it is planted in the shade as an understory tree, its crown is narrow, but if it reaches the sun the crown spreads out, luxuriating in the light. The wood is hard and heavy with a specific gravity of 0.9.

It likes moist, nutrient-rich soils with a wide PH tolerance and grows at a moderate rate in tropical hammocks. It can take flooding, but not long-term water. If the soil is rich the tree may get taller. The largest specimen is the National Champion Tree in Miami that has a circumference of 73 inches and a height of 41 feet with a crown spread of 34 feet.

Despite liking moist soils, the tree is tolerant of short periods of drought. It hates the cold and drops its leaves if it is too cold. It needs to be planted away from salt winds, but can take some wind abuse and survive.

It is my experience that Satinleaf is a bit tricky to plant, and needs to be watered for a longer time when transplanted. In my gardens, once it was established, it thrived without special watering.

Caterpillars eat its leaves, but do no permanent damage to the plant. Leaf-notchers take chunks out of the leaves. It can get gall mite. The Mediterranean fruit fly also shows up at times. Key Deer do not eat the leaves.

Key West Garden Club and McCoy Indigenous Park have this specimen tree. Its leaves are a dead-giveaway to identification.

You would think that there would be plenty of these flirty girls around, but although there is a Satinwood Island in the Everglades, she is listed as threatened by the State of Florida.

Seagrape *(Coccoloba uvifera)*

Crazy Coccoloba - A Tropical Treasure

Protected from winds in the interior, the seagrape *(Cocoloba uvifera)* could reach anyplace from 10 to 50 feet in height. Check out the one at 900 Flagler Avenue to see a huge tree, carefully pruned by landscape architect Debra Yates. It looks as though it is a giant's bonsai.

However, in the Keys it is usually found along coastal areas and since high winds associated with storms snap its brittle branches, the tree often remains low and is as wide as it is high. Chances are, that if it is shaped by the winds, this cutie often will look more like a ten-foot bush with round bangles clanking around her limbs than a tree.

Round leaves that can grow up to seven inches across make this specimen one of the most unusual trees inhabiting the Keys. Leaves emerge from a stipule that wraps around the branch. Leaves are a soft and sensuous bronzed-pink when they emerge, then they harden to bright green with red veins and stems and finally transform to brilliant russet-red. Floating like Frisbees to the ground, they slowly dry, coating the ground with a pale brown rug.

Draw or write messages on their dry smooth surfaces with colored sharpies. Pull out your acrylics and paint invitations to a beach party on the dry surfaces or if you are less creative, write your grocery list on one. Before drying, their red colors make a striking addition to a flower arrangement. *Coccoloba* is in the Polygonaceae (Buckwheat) Family, the same as pigeon plum.

Thin, splotchy bark covers the seagrape's massive, two-foot in diameter trunk that expands into stout branches. Kids love climbing their sturdy limbs. Branches that are cut off and planted and will grow into a new tree, although they will not be as strong as a tree grown from seed. Cutting the lower branches could damage the tree.

In the summer, seagrapes bloom with small, white flowers on long panicles. These turn

52

into deep purple grapes in the late summer. Each grape has a large seed in the center. Not every tree will have fruit, as there are male and female trees and only the female trees produce fruit.

The bunch of seagrape fruit ripens unevenly so in order to harvest them, (if you can get there before the birds eat them) place a large sheet under the fruit and shake the tree. The ripe grapes will fall to the ground and you can scoop them up in the sheet. Jellies, jams and wine can be made from the fruit.

Seagrape Jelly
1-quart sea grape juice
5 tablespoons lemon or limejuice
1 package powdered pectin
5 cups sugar

To prepare juice: Wash sea grapes and measure. Put in fairly large, wide pot with half as much water (1 cup water to 2 cups sea grapes). Bring to a boil. Mash often with a potato masher and continue boiling until fruit is reduced to a soft pulp (about 25 to 30 minutes). Drain through a jelly bag or several layers of cheesecloth. Do not squeeze.

Place one-quart of juice in a wide kettle. Turn heat high and add lemon or lime juice and pectin. Bring mixture to a rolling boil. Stir in sugar and return to a rolling boil. Boil hard for one minute, stirring constantly. Remove from heat. Skim foam if necessary. Pour into hot, sterilized jars, leaving a quarter-inch headspace. Adjust caps. Process five minutes in boiling water bath. (If you use unripe seagrapes as well as ripe ones you can eliminate the pectin.)

Many species are fond of the sea grape. They provide significant food and cover for wildlife and are nectar sources for the Florida duskywing *(Ephyriades brunneus,)* Julia *(dryas iulia)* and Schaus' swallowtail *(Papilio aristodemus ponceanus)* butterflies.

Seagrape will withstand salt-water inundation, drought, salt winds and sandy, well-drained soil and it thrives in full sun. A freeze will damage the tree so they are not found further north.

Medicinally, a gum from the bark was used for treating throat ailments and the roots for treating dysentery. The wood is prized for cabinets and, if it is boiled, makes a red dye. In landscaping, seagrapes can be pruned to be a hedge or a fence. Many have been planted at Ft. Zachary Taylor State Park and there is a hedgerow of them across from Smather's Beach in Key West.

Seven-year apple *(Genipa clusiifolia)*

Hardy Seven-Year Apple - Denizen of the Beach

Ironically, the seven-year apple *(Genipa clusiifolia)* is neither an apple nor does it take seven years for it to mature. It is in the Rubiaceae Family. This leathery denizen of beachfronts manages to flower and form fruit at the same time, which is a good thing because it takes ten months for the fruit to ripen. When it does ripen, it is devoured by mockingbirds that hollow out the ripened fruit and leave a dead skin hanging in the tree. Butterflies, such as the Tantalus sphinx *(Aeliopus tantalus)* consume it as a larval host plant and the mangrove skipper *(Phocides pigmalion)* and others consume its nectar.

This small tree grows well along the coastline. Although it can't take sitting in salt water like the mangrove, it does well directly on the coastline where it gets inundated with storm water. It does surprisingly well with heavy winds and comes back with new leaves on a dense rounded crown. The bark is smooth and pale.

Seven-year apples have six-inch, shiny, leaves that curl inward. They are thick, a long oval, and clustered near the branch tips. It has a five-petaled cluster of pink edged white flowers that emerge mostly in the spring and early summer, but can be found all year long. Male and female flowers are on different plants. The flowers have a magnificent smell and could easily be used in perfume; *Eau de Genipa* could be a big seller.

Fruits emerge as a hard, green pear-shaped orb two to three inches long, and hang on the tree while they turn yellow, dark brown and then black. When they are dark brown they are ready to eat, but beware of the many seeds. They are probably best left to the mockingbirds. These seeds are prolific and can be propagated easily.

The natives are only found in the southern-most tip of Florida, Sanibel Island and in the Caribbean. A slow grower, often they are as wide as they are tall reaching a top height of fifteen feet. It grows in part shade and sun, but I have only seen them thrive in full sun. Soil must be porous; sand and rocks are ideal. Alkaline limestone will do just fine. They survive in the second tier away from a beach. Their drought tolerance is high. Because seven-year apple is native, there are no life-threatening pests found on the plant.

If you plant them close together, they will make a full hedge or screen. They are great as windbreaks near the ocean. Although the fruits are fairly ugly the flowers are showy and they would make lovely specimen shrubs. They can withstand median strip planting or survive in a parking lot island. Try growing them in large pots on the patio or balcony as they can take the strong ocean winds.

Although they are not seven-year fruit, nor apples, they do hold a strong niche in the Keys environment. If you want to see one take a look out at Ft. Zachary Taylor State Park as you come into the park near the Navy's chain link fence.

Smooth Strongback (*Bourreria succulenta*)

Endangered Smooth Strongback Perfumes the Air

Roger L. Hammer, the renowned botanist, was speaking with a Bahamian restauranteur about bush medicine when the confusion between the names smooth Bahama strongbark and smooth strongback came up. She told him that women make a tea from the leaves to give their husbands a "strong back." When he asked if that was for lifting things she replied with great laughter, "Oh, no, no, no, mon!"

The *Bourreria succelenta* is also known as bodywood or pigeon berry. It is fairly common in Keys rockland hammocks, but the rest of Florida should be jealous as it is rare in other places. Its aromatic ½-inch, white blossoms fill the breezes with perfume all year, but peak in the summer and fall. You'll recognize it by its bright red drupe of berries and those fragrant little white flowers.

This is a large shrub or small tree with vine-like droopy branches that cascade towards the ground. Its oval, three-inch, shiny-green leaves have a notched or rounded tip. They are green with orange tinted ribs. With moderate growth, normally it doesn't get more than 20 feet high, 15 feet wide and six-inches in circumference, but in 1999, Joseph Nemac, a park ranger at Key Largo Hammock Botanical State Park, is credited with finding a smooth strongback in Monroe County that is 33 feet in height and has a 17 foot spread.

This tree is a native so, as usual, it loves the nutrient-poor soil; it can survive long droughts and has made it through 50-mile-per-hour winds in my gardens. It likes full sun but does well with light shade, too. It has few pests or diseases. Smooth strongback can be propagated from de-pulped and scarified seeds.

Smooth strongback has some cousins around town. Some 'rough' strongback (B. radula) specimens are at the Key West Cemetery near the "I told you I was sick" gravestone. A third rare member of this family in the Keys, the little pineland strongback (B. cassinifolia) is a lacy bush with orange fruit.

Soapberry *(Sapindus saponaria)*

Soapberry Seedpods Yield Suds

The soapberry or winged soapberry tree (*Sapindus saponaria*) has bright green leaves, but its dark brown berry is greener than any of its leaves. I speak in riddles. How can brown be green?

The brown seedpods of the soapberry tree create an organic natural soap when added to water. There are over 2,000 species of the Sapindaceae Family but only 13 species within the genus Sapindus. Whereas the species found in India and China, *S. mukorossi,* is the tree primarily used for production of the commercial natural products associated with the seedpods, our own native soapberry has a lesser talent for suds production. Seedpods must be soaked for three days to produce suds.

In Asia and across the Americas, soapnuts have been used for washing for thousands of years. They have commercial uses in cosmetics and detergents. Mixed in water, they will clean your car, your glasses your jewelry and your body. If you dump the used soapy water or throw the nutshells on the ground, they repel insects.

An ancient book, *Indica* by Megasthenes, a Greek traveler in 302 B.C., describes soapberry use. "In India, Kings & Queens have used clean hygienic fragrance cloths. I am amazed that the soaps are grown in trees."

Even more amazing for Key West, "kernel extracts of the nut disrupt the activity of enzymes of larva and pupae and inhibit the growth of the *Aedes aegypti,* the mosquito that spreads dengue fever," according to the online January 18, 2011 issue of *Acta Tropica.*

The small tree can reach a height of 15 to 20 feet in the Keys. The light brown wood is hard and tough and the bark is gray. Large flakes expose reddish-brown under bark. It is an understory hammock tree preferring light shade to full sun. It grows in nutrient poor soil, but likes some organic material. Soapberry is moderately salt-wind and drought tolerant, but it does not like inundation by brackish water.

This tree is easily recognizable because of its unusual leaf structure. The leaves are pinnately compound and contain four to nine inch, lance-shaped leaflets that are two to four inches long. They are on winged rachis, which means that the leaf appears to grow all the way down the stem like narrow wings.

Hundreds of tiny, white flowers burst into bloom in terminal clusters and turn the tree into a fragrant triangular-shaped cornucopia. They become one-half-inch, yellowish-orange berries that fade to brown as they age. Jewelry is created from the shiny, black seeds called black pearls found inside the pods. These seeds are said to be poisonous.

The name *Sapindus* is derived from two Latin words, *saponis,* which means soap and *indicus,* which means from India. Saponins are toxic to cold-blooded vertebrates but not to warm-blooded animals. Clever natives threw crushed soapberry fruits into the water to stupefy fish so that they floated to the surface for easy gathering.

Soapberry trees attract bees and other wildlife and will give the grower little cause for concern. Seedlings are often found beneath the tree as well as root suckers.

In folk medicine, it is used to treat excess mucus or salivation, epilepsy and tumors. It has anti-microbial characteristics. Modern medicine investigated it to treat migraines and vaginal Candida. It has some contraceptive capability, but is not reliable. Ayervedic medicine uses soapberries to treat eczema, psoriasis and to remove freckles. Its insecticidal properties are reputed to remove lice from hair. Users throw the seedpods on their gardens as they discourage insects. Seedpods can be ordered over the Internet, but caution must be exercised to make sure that you are not getting the seeds as well as the pods and that you are getting *S. mukorossi.* Do not plant these seeds; plant the native *Sapindus saponaria.*

The Keys soapberry tree is found mostly above Lignumvitae Key. Good examples can be found in the Crane Point Hammock, and at Fort Zachary Taylor behind the concession stand.

Using soapberry seeds to wash will make you as green as you can get.

Spanish Stopper (*Eugenia foetida*)

Confab with Frothy Fairies on the Spanish Stopper

The white flowers of the Spanish stopper (*Eugenia foetida*) cluster around the branches of the tree creating froth that looks like a confab of tiny fairies. Every fairy breath flings fragrance into the air with abandon. When the wind catches the branches the fairies dance a Spanish fandango.

Like the magical people of the Keys, it can juggle several jobs at the same time, both flowering and fruiting. The small, edible berries turn orange and then black and provide food for a variety of birds. Key deer do not like to eat the leaves.

The leathery, dark-green leaves have no veins seen in the leaf. But their shape, oval, one to two inches long and dark green color often gets them the common name box leaf stopper. They have fine black dots on the undersides. The tree is evergreen with leaves remaining to the second year. The round, white flowers are fragrant. *Eugenia* means flowering for this plant in the Myrtaceae Family. This is an understory tree 8 to 15 feet in height.

The stopper has a root system that allows it to grow in the most difficult places, such as a crack in a rock. Like all natives, give the tree some rubble, clay or rocky soil, but good compost and mulch will make it thrive. Drought tolerant, salt-wind tolerant and often able to withstand a short inundation of salt water makes the stopper a highly desirable tree.

The plant is used as an accent shrub or small tree and is often a pioneering plant in coastal hammocks and thickets. Accustomed to growing under taller trees, it doesn't need full sun. Several slim, erect trunks grow to create an irregularly-rounded crown. The trunk gets concentric circles on the bark when older. Orange under-bark shows up when the older bark peels away. The tree can be trimmed to display the beautiful bark on the many trunks.

The name 'stopper' refers to its folkloric medicinal uses. The reddish bark makes a tea that was used to treat diarrhea. There are few life-threatening pests or diseases that affect it.

Many butterflies love the stopper's nectar-attracting flowers, especially the long-lived, Zebra longwing *(Heliconius charitonius,)* Florida's state butterfly.

Because of their many small branches, stoppers can be used as hedges or screens, street trees, or even as a specimen trees. The growth rate is moderate. The largest one on the American Forests: National Register of Big Trees' website is 25 feet tall with a nine foot spread and 12 inches in circumference found in 1999 by Joseph Nemec in Monroe County.

Propagated from seeds, it takes a couple of months before germinating. For indoor gardeners, it is a good candidate for bonsai. The University of Florida says that the plant "has outstanding ornamental features and could be planted more." It can be seen at the Key West Garden Club.

Spicewood Tree *Calyptranthes pallens*)

Exotic Aromas Encourage Clipping the Spicewood Hedge

You don't have to go to the jungles of Brazil to find new anti-cancer drugs. In addition to the rainforest, Key West has its own native pharmacy of medicines in the spicewood tree (*Calyptranthes pallens.*) The University of Illinois at Chicago has researched the anti-cancer effects of a chemical that they found in its leaves and twigs that is active against human oral carcinoma.

The Cherokee tribe made a tea from its branches sweetened with honey that they called *ah-dee-tah-stee.* They used it to treat upset stomachs and sleeplessness. Revolutionary War soldiers drank it when they ran out of coffee. They might have had a few upset tummies and a bit of sleeplessness, too.

This multi-trunked, tree/shrub grows at a moderate rate to 20 feet in height by ten feet in width as undergrowth in hardwood hammocks. Beautiful pale-burgundy baby leaves emerge before they slowly turn a dark green. When young, they are covered with rusty hairs to discourage predators from eating them. Full grown, the leaves are two and one half inches long, dense, compact, evergreen and opposite. When they are crushed they smell exotically spicy. Who needs showy flowers when there are leaves like this? You can take pride in planting it.

Its tiny, white flowers are inconspicuous in the spring, but their fragrance forms a cloud that hovers around the branches. The flowers are bisexual and polygamous, if you like to think about these things. Young smooth bark becomes scaly as it ages, just like us. It attracts bees and butterflies.

Many species of birds delight in the small round fruit of this desirable Myrtaceae Family plant, the same family as stoppers. It will attract the versatile voices of the mockingbirds, cardinals and woodpeckers. The fruit turns from green to yellow, then red to black. Small birds take cover in the thick foliage and bees and butterflies are attracted to the flowers.

Spicewood can be trained to be either a tree or a shrub. It thrives in partial shade or full sun and can take damp soil, but once established, is drought tolerant. Nutrient poor soils are its equivalent of our broccoli although it thrives with humus-filled topsoil. Salt wind may burn its leaves so don't plant it right on the ocean. It is an understory plant in the rockland hammocks. Spicewood has no major pests or diseases and is definitely a xeriscaping star.

This plant may be used as a specimen or planted as a superior hedge. Pruning it would be a pleasure as it perfumes the air with spice when its leaves are cut. As a small tree, it can be used in parking lots or median strips in highways. That means it's tough. It will survive the hurricanes. It would be good sun cover for a window air conditioner.

A specimen can be seen at the Key West Garden Club. Do not mistake it for spicebush, (*Lendera benzoin*) or myrtle-of-the river *(Calyptranthes zuzygium)* two totally different plants with similar common names.

Strangler Fig *(Ficus aurea)*

Womb to Tomb Inflorescence for the Gall Wasp

Take the strangler fig, a plant that never ceases to amaze in its variety and adaptations. It begins its life as a tiny seed deposited by a variety of birds. Since the rain forest doesn't allow much sunlight on the forest floor, the strangler fig seed opts for the sunlight at the top of a host tree. The seed lands in the top of a tree, maybe a cabbage palm, and although an unwelcome guest, begins to annihilate its host.

It grows slowly at first, but soon puts down roots that begin to wrap around the trunk of its host tree. As soon as the roots hit the ground and access nutrients from the soil, the strangler fig has a growth spurt. Think of the poor cabbage palm as being encased in a woven Chinese finger trap. The trap gets tighter and tighter and it becomes harder and harder to breathe as the fig squeezes off the nutrients to its host both in its trunk and its roots. The crown of the fig grows foliage that soon blocks the sun from the host tree. Its waxy, ovoid leaves are three to five inches long and protect the tree from drying winds and excessive sun. They are larval food for the ruddy daggerwing butterflies *(Marpesia petreus.)* The strangler fig can grow up to 40 feet in height with an umbrella-shaped canopy.

The host tree dies, leaving a hollow center totally surrounded by the encapsulating fig. There are a thousand different species of these figs in the world, all hard at work in the killing fields

64

where they are considered "keystone" plants because they are so important to the animals of the forest. Strangler figs in the Keys are an important food source supplying food for migrating birds. Endangered white-crowned pigeons are gluttons for the fruit. The tree provides homes for thousands of invertebrates as well as rodents, bats, and birds.

If this murderous lifestyle is not enough to satisfy your horticultural voyeurism, its sex life is even more bizarre. The way that a fig gets sexual fulfillment would not be believed if it were transformed from a tree to a young dryad nymph.

There are no flowers visible on the tree. Both the male and two varieties of female flowers are inside a hollow fruit (cyconia). The males carry pollen and the females, seed. One female has a long style and the other a short style. (Think about how long it took for this plant to evolve all of these attributes.)

Now enters the pollinator through a two-mm orifice in the bottom of the cyconia where the tiny, female wasp (*Pegascarpus jimenezi*) loses her wings. Each wasp species is specific to one species of fig tree. She won't need wings any more as this is her tomb as well as her womb. She lays her eggs in the neuter ovary of the short-styled female flower and being of no further use, dies.

The male wasp hatches first and has a short, but sexually-charged life. His first job is to bite a hole in the female flower ovary and inseminate the new female wasp. Before he dies, he chews an exit hole in the cyconia for the female. The female wasp crawls over the pollen laden flowers, leaves the cyconia and repeats the birthing process to pollinate the fig tree. She is born, impregnated as an infant, flies to another cynconia and enters it as a mother-to-be, lays eggs and dies, living a brief but significant life. Without her carrying pollen from one cyconia to another there would be no fig trees.

As D.H. Lawrence wrote in his poem "Figs": "Every fruit has its secret/ the fig is a very secretive fruit…The flowering turned all inward and womb-fibrilled;/ And but one orifice."

The fig tree can withstand high, salty winds, salt-water inundation, and nutrient-poor soil. It fruits all year long. Figs grow quickly and are semi-deciduous, with leaves falling in the spring. The bark is gray and smooth. Wood was used for arrows and bows, aerial roots as cords and fishing lines. There is a glowing example of it devouring the bricks in the Key West Garden Club. If you find this epiphyte in the branches of your tree, rip it out before it commits horticultural murder.

Don't lock your bike to a fig as Shel Silverstein did before he died. The strangler fig will eat it. All we can see of the bike today is a wee corner of the basket.

Sweet Acacia *(Acacia farnesiana)*

Sweet Acacia Flaunts Dangerous Thorns

Frederic Malle Une Fleur de Cassie, a perfume created by Dominique Ropion in 2003, harnesses the aroma of the sweet acacia flowers. He describes it as "the warm and powdery fragrance of the cassie flowers, their spicy cinnamon facets underscored by balsamic undertones. The woody base notes are smooth and polished, like a necklace of pale beads one can buy from wood carver's stalls in the Indian markets."

The sweet acacia was brought to Europe's Cardinal Odoardo Farnese (1573-1626) from the West Indies and planted in one of the first gardens in Rome, the Farnese Estate's Botanical Gardens in 1611.

At the turn of the century, the fragrant flowers of sweet acacia *(Acacia farnesiana)* bloomed in the south of France where they were distilled into oils and sent to Grasse to become expensive little bottles of olfactory joy. In the Old Testament (2nd Book Moses, Ch 30, 22-26) God tells Moses to prepare a holy oil from Myrrh, cinnamon, rose water and Kassia. When the perfumeries in France began to create an essence from sweet acacia they named it cassie, in a reference to this quote.

Now most of the trees are cultivated in India where labor is less expensive.

A native, 15-foot tree grows as large horizontally as it does vertically. It is covered with fine alternately arranged leaves that are bipinnately compound. They resemble mimosa leaves and the compound leaves of the Fabaceae Family. The two-inch leaflets dance on the breeze in a light, feathery green outfit.

Despite the sweet-smelling, yellow puffball flower and the graceful leaves, the slightly zigzagged, brown twigs and branches are armed with white, vicious-looking, one-inch thorns. Acacia is the Greek word for thorn. It is not a good tree for inquisitive children.

In its favor, it blooms frequently year-round and bees love its nectar. The Department of Agriculture's Forest Service recommends that lower branches be pruned to develop a strong structure.

The Key West sweet acacia tree likes full sun, well-drained soil and is drought tolerant. If it gets too dry it will shed its leaves. The Forest Service says that few pests are seen on the tree but it is used as nesting cover for wildlife. If planted, its unusual looks might provoke more than a few questions about its nature and origin.

Sweet acacia is made into oils used for tanning, ink, glue and of course, perfume. The seeds are edible and are 17% protein. They grow in three-inch pods that curl on the branches. They begin green and ripen to a dark brown. In traditional medicine, sweet acacia has been used to treat malaria, diarrhea and skin diseases.

There are more than 1,000 kinds of acacias throughout the world, but only one is native to the Keys. The largest sweet acacia on record in America is found in Texas and is 29 feet high, with a 43-foot spread and a circumference of 160 inches.

The sweet-flowered, needle-bush certainly has contradictory tendencies.

White Mangrove *(Laguncularia racemosa)*

White Mangrove: Not Related to Black or Red Mangrove

The white mangrove *(Laguncularia racemosa)* reaches about 30-feet in height with a narrow, rounded crown. It is taller than it is wide, usually existing above the high-tide line, further back from the shoreline than the unrelated species of red or black mangrove. Frequently, they all grow closely together with the unrelated buttonwood getting in the mix as well. In the Keys, white mangrove needs nutrient-rich soil and full sun to grow to 15 to 20 feet in height.

The white mangrove typically has no visible aerial root but if inundated with salt water can grow modified pneumatophores similar to the black mangrove or prop roots like the red mangrove. They do not persist as long. Its bark is thick, reddish-brown and scaly. The tree is not drought tolerant.

The leaves are different from the other two mangrove trees. The opposite dark-green, oval leaves are leathery and succulent. Unlike the pointy leaves on the other two mangroves, these are rounded at the base. They are one to three inches long and sometimes notched at the tip. There are two glands at the base of the leaf blade. They are not salt glands but nectar glands. When the leaves are new, these nectar glands produce sweet nectar that many insects find yummy. The presence of the insects that feed on the nectar helps to protect the tree from other insects that are pests.

The leaves have air pockets around the underside-edge of the leaf. They can close these pores as well. In a symbiotic relationship, mites inhabit these pores. Because their leaves often become covered with salt, they look whitish; some say that is why they are called their common name, white mangrove. If white mangroves are exposed to a significant amount of salt they exclude it through their root systems.

The fragrant, small whitish-green flowers have five velvety petals. They grow in clusters on terminal spikes. Small ants and wasps pollinate them.

There are two kinds of sexual reproduction for these trees. One tree has male and female flowers on the same tree. However, the further south the mangrove grows, the more trees we find that are only male. This is called androdioecious. Only nine other plant species in the world have this quality.

The fruit are greenish-brown with ten ribs like a pumpkin, and only one seed inside. The half-inch seedpods turn dark red and germinate while still on the tree. Eventually, it drops into the sediment where it is transported by tides and currents. It can remain viable for a year or more.

The Latin scientific name of the tree *Laguncularia* means a little flask. *Racemosa* means cluster and refers to the growth pattern of the fruit that clusters on terminal stems.

Many birds, some with declining populations or labeled endangered, use the three varieties of mangroves for nesting and feeding. Roseate spoonbills, limpkins, white ibis, herons, bitterns, anhingas, osprey, peregrine falcons and bald eagles are examples.

As with the red and black mangrove, the white mangrove protects and stabilizes low-lying coastal areas. It provides food sources and protection for coastal fish. The tannin in the bark is used as a dye and medicinally to treat fevers, ulcers, dysentery, scurvy and tumors in folk medicine. In the past the trees were used as fuel, and for furniture, boats, fence posts and tools.

Florida Statute, Chapter 403, regulates trimming mangroves. Prior to any trimming, the Florida Department of Environmental Protection should be consulted. You must obtain a permit and hire a certified arborist. You can see white mangrove behind the fence at 1500 Atlantic Boulevard and along North Roosevelt Boulevard.

Wild Dilly *(Manilkara jaimiqui ssp. emarginata)*

National Champion Wild Dilly Tree in Key West

The not for profit American Forests maintains the National Register of Big Trees. These trees are the largest specimens that have been reported to the organization. The report must include the span of the crown of the tree, the height and the circumference. These three numbers are totaled to determine whether the tree is the largest and a champion. These numbers can go into a thousand for some mammoth U.S. specimens.

Here in the Keys however, due to our high winds from tropical storm and hurricane events and nutrient-poor soils, the trees are considerably smaller. Native, threatened wild dilly *(Manilkara jaimiqui* ssp. *emarginata)* is located in the Key West Botanical Gardens. It has the distinction of being the current National Champion wild dilly. The total score is a 68.

This is how it is figured out. Take one-quarter of the size of the crown of the tree. Add that to the total height of the tree. You can get the height using fancy equipment called a clinometer, which measures the incline from about 150 feet, and using a mathematical formula, figures out that our champion wild dilly is exactly 24 feet tall. Then measure the circumference at exactly four-and-one-half-feet from the ground, a measurement known as the dbh or diameter at breast height and total. (If you have a nominee and you need an application form, research American Forests: Register of National Trees.)

The Florida Keys have over 110 different species of trees, more than anywhere north of Mexico. We have quite a few of the national champions that will only grow in the tropical and subtropical environments found in the Florida Keys. Key West is reputed to have 12 of them.

The wild dilly in the Botanical Gardens was moved from the Sugarloaf school development site and is doing well in the courtyard gardens. It took a long time to get this big. It is a very slow-growing, understory tree that typically reaches 10 to 15 feet in height. This species is found in coastal berm and coastal rock barren habitats. It is less common in the interior of the hammock. Its densely rounded crown contains dark-green leaves that are thick and leathery. They are two to four inches long, oblong, and notched at the apex. They grow in clusters at the terminal ends of the branches.

The reddish wood is heavy and dense like the sapodilla tree, and other members of its Sapotaceae Family. When the wood is exposed to air it gradually darkens to a deep russet. Like most natives, it survives salt-water inundations, but not long term. It usually thrives in the interior of the hammock so its leaves may burn when exposed to salt wind. The wild dilly likes nutrient-poor, well-drained, limestone soil but with a top layer of humus. It can withstand drought once established.

Six-lobed, one half-inch clusters of yellowish flowers occur frequently year round. The flowers are followed by a one half to one inch, light brown, globular berry. When the scruffy berry ripens to a light brown, and the juice is thick, it is edible and like the sapodilla fruit is chewy, like gum. Inside are several black seeds. This chewing gum was introduced to the United States by General Antonio Lopez de Santa Anna in 1866.

The name *Manilkara* is derived from the word for the genus in India. *Jai-mi-ki* means water crab spirit in the language of the Taino Indians. Other words acquired from the Taino are yucca, iguana and hurricane. Mayans chewed the fruit. Caribbean islanders make syrup from the berries. Wild dilly tree is native to the US.

Wild dilly attracts wildlife looking for food and cover as well as insects to pollinate it. Plant this splendid native tree and become entitled to bragging rights.

Wild Lime, Prickly-ash *(Zanthoxylum fagara)*

Wild Lime Cat-claw Hooks Await Human Invaders

Pity the poor surveyors of Flagler's railroad when they were struggling through the native Keys vegetation and they came to a thicket of wild limes. The mosquitoes might have been horrendous, but other formidable adversaries lay in wait, tempting the men with their lushly-lime perfumed leaves. The thorns on the wild lime, *(Zanthoxylum fagara)* could rip them apart, not to mention create nasty skin irritations. In human terms, this plant would be classified as a monster but for wild life it is marvelous.

This multi-trunk, tree/bush can grow to 15 feet in height and 12 feet in width. It has small irregularly shaped branches embedded with sharp hooked spines. Its leaves are odd-pinnate each containing 7 to 15 inch-long leaflets. In Spanish, wild lime is called *una de gatos,* in reference to a female cat's sharp claws. Small, compound, bright-green leaves adorn the branches of this native plant.

Sadly, they have no limes, but they do attract the caterpillar of the giant swallowtail butterfly *(Papilio cresphontes)* that much prefers their leaves to their secondary choice, your Key lime tree. The caterpillars look like bird droppings, but a six and a half inch wingspan gives the yellow and black butterfly A+ garden credentials. The wild lime also attracts the rare, federally threatened Schaus' swallowtail butterfly *(Heraclides aristodemus ponceanus.)* Deer also like to nibble wild lime leaves.

While a wild lime thicket is impenetrable to humans, it is also impenetrable to predatory animals, resulting in excellent nesting sites for small birds. The nectar from the small, yellow flower attracts insects. Inside the wild lime's small, brown, paired fruits is a black seed. It attracts both fruit-eating and insect-eating birds.

Seminoles made bows and arrows from the wood. They used the plant to treat stomach aches, to increase circulation, as a stimulant, a diuretic and to treat syphilis.

Zanthoxylum, the scientific name, means yellow in Greek. The wood produces a yellow dye and the tiny stem-mounted flowers are also yellow and bloom off and on all year. The black fruit is contained in orange-brown follicles. The word *fagara* is related to pepper. Some species of Zanthoxylum seeds are used as a spicy condiment, especially in Indian and Chinese cooking. They are not eaten, but removed before serving, like bay leaves.

If this wild lime is planted right next to the shore it will lose its leaves in high winds. It does not kill the tree however and the leaves return after a month or so. Once it is established and it can thrive in nutrient poor soils with high PH and little water. It likes full sun, but can tolerate shade. Wild lime has no serious pests. This inexpensive tree is our kind of xeriscaping plant.

There aren't many of these around the city that are grown-ups. Look for one at Ft. Zachary Taylor near the entrance to the fort and at the Key West Garden Club. These are inexpensive trees.

The wild lime is used as a buffer strip between homes or on highway medians. This lacy plant combined with some yucca would keep everything but wildlife at bay, so if you have a fence that you don't want people to climb, plant a wild lime.

Wild Tamarind (*Lysiloma latisiliquum*)

Rare Wild Tamarind - A Lollapalooza of a Native Tree

The wild tamarind (*Lysiloma latisiliquum*) is a lollapalooza of a native tree. Completing the tamarind trio is the non-native Guatemalan and Bahamian tamarind, but do not confuse them with the Indian tamarind tree that has edible pulp around its seeds and is used in Worchestershire sauce, Indian cooking, and Caribbean sweets. The edible variety can be found in the Audubon House garden. The common name comes from '*tamar*' which means dried date and '(h)*ind*' which refers to India.

The wild tamarind tree's pods are definitely not edible. They are much shorter, only four to five inches long, and have a rather distinctive thin, brown and white pod that turns gradually to deep dark brown. It is flat, but sometimes twisted on the ends and contains eight to ten hard, oval shiny seeds about a half-inch long. Our native wild tamarind is quite rare in the lower Keys and is native to Big Pine Key. When hit together, the seedpods make the same castanet sounds of other plants in the Fabacaea Family.

Usually reaching forty feet in height, the wild tamarind provides excellent shade. It is a major canopy tree in rockland hammocks. The American Forests: National Register of Big Trees' website project lists the largest that was found in Monroe County at 58 feet tall, 85 inches in circumference with a spread of 44 feet. The trunk can grow to three feet in diameter and on older trees has a flat scaling bark. The bark is in strong contrast to its wispy, compound obovate (oval) leaflets that look a lot like the leaves of a Poinciana tree except that the branches drape gracefully downward like a ballerina's limbs.

Native tree woodworkers like this dark, rare wood because of its interesting grains, similar to black walnut, that reflect the light, changing from golden hues to brown. Many woodworkers find their tamarind after hurricanes. Once, local woodworker Jack Keppler, found a forty-four inch wild tamarind with a thirty-inch hole in the center. This tree rotted when water got into its pith after a branch snapped off. Termites and carpenter ants ate it. Not one to waste, he made coffee table bases from the circular wood.

Tiny, half-inch, white puffballs cover the tree in the spring and on through the fall and are very fragrant. They attract much wildlife, from the cassius blue (*Lepototes cassius*) and large orange sulphur (*Colias eurytheme*) butterflies to the endangered, native Stock Island tree snail (*Orthalicus reses*), which affix themselves to the smooth bark of the young trees. These snails must conserve water during the dry months, so they create a watertight seal between the bark and themselves. Look for their brown and white shell with ringed stripes about head high and upwards on the trunk. Birds also like these trees, especially our migrating warblers. They are attracted to the insects that are present because of the sap formed from the new leaf development and the insects that are attracted to the flowers.

Being a native, the sun-loving tree can grow in nutrient-poor, salty soil, is drought tolerant and moderately salt-wind tolerant. The new, young leaves are a redolent red, which show off against the light green of the older leaves. Few pests or diseases attack this native.

The State of Florida says that wild tamarind has outstanding ornamental features and should be planted more in the lower Keys because it is such a useful shade tree. It could be used in parking lots and as street plantings because its roots are not a problem. As it is evergreen, it is an excellent quick-growing specimen tree for yards or public parks.

There is a Wild Tamarind Trail at John Pennekamp Coral Reef State park that is a twenty-minute walk through numerous native trees. The tree also can be seen behind Schooner Wharf in Key West. If the wild tamarind is in tune with your tastes, it could play its castanets in your front yard.

Willow Bustic *(Sideroxylon salicifolium)*

The Willow Bustic Grows Out of Its Teenage Bumps.

Heavy clusters of warty, pod-like bumps form on the young stems of the native willow bustic tree *(Sideroxylon salicifolium)* like an outbreak of pimples on a teenager. Any normal person would think that some horrid sap-eating insect had infected this tree, but a far fancier answer awaits the patient gardener. The ugly eruptions at the leaf axis burst into dozens of fragrant white flowers about a quarter-inch across, usually in the spring, but they bloom from May to November.

The leaves are dark green on top and pale underneath and shaped like lances. The five-inch leaves grow alternate to each other on the stem and are crowded on the ends of the branches. New leaves emerge a peachy orange color.

The willow bustic is self-sufficient sexually. Both male and female flowers are formed on the same tree so it doesn't need another tree around it to make it complete. The flowers smell a bit like grape jelly and attract the best butterflies.

After flowering the plant produces small dark fruit that are manna to the birds. The fruits begin green, turn rusty-red and end as tasty black morsels. Cardinals, mockingbirds, jays and many migrating birds gorge themselves on the quarter-inch berries. Some of our flying seed distributors also nest in the tree. That makes the commute to the grocery store very convenient. The fruits are reputed to be tasty, even to humans.

The flowers attract the imperiled Florida duskywing *(Ephyriades brunneus floridensis)* the red banded hairstreak *(Calycopis cecrop)* and many other butterflies. The Florida leafwing butterfly

76

(*Anaea troglodyta floridensis*) feeds on the sap after yellow-bellied sapsuckers create a feeding hole. Caterpillars sometimes defoliate it.

Willow bustic is in the Sapodilla Family and the word "sapota" comes from the Nahuatl language, spoken by the Aztecs, and was Latinized by Carl Linnaeus, the Swedish botanist responsible for the system of how plants are named. *Sideroxylon* means iron wood. The word *salicifolia* is divided into two sections, *salici* means willow-like. *Folia* means leaf.

The leaves are shaped like the lanky lance-shaped leaf of the willow growing to six inches in length. They are shiny on the top and dull underneath and grow alternately on the stem.

The willow bustic tree grows at a moderate rate usually attaining 30 feet in height with a rounded crown. Lower branches drop off as it grows. The American Forests: National Register of Big Trees' website lists one that is 57 feet high, with a 54-inch circumference and a spread of 18 feet.

The bark begins smooth and then matures to a flaky cover. Willow bustic is native to South Florida and throughout the Caribbean. It is a common understory species in the upper Keys hammocks, but is suffering from a lack of the Florida hammock landscape that it loves.

It grows well once established. It does not need any supplemental water, likes the full sun or full shade, and can grow in nutrient-poor soils. It prefers to be protected from salt wind and water.

The willow bustic is a native, accent tree that is sure to evoke neighborly comment when it bursts into bloom.

Index

Acacia farnesiana, 66
Avicennia germinans, 8
Blackbead, 4
Black Ironwood, 6
Black Mangrove, 8
Blolly, 10
Bourreria succulenta, 56
Bursera simaruba, 22
Buttonwood, 12
Calyptranthes pallens, 62
Canella winterana, 14
Capparis cynophallophora, 26
Chrysophyllum oliviforme, 50
Cinnamon Bark, 14
Citharexylum spinosum, 18
Coccoloba diversifolia, 44
Coccoloba uvifera, 52
Conocarpus erectus, 12
Cordia sebestena, 20
Drypetes diversifolia, 36
Eugenia foetida, 60
Exothea paniculata, 24
False Mastic, 16
Ficus aurea, 64
Fiddlewood, 18
Geiger Tree, 20
Genipa clusiifolia, 54
Guaiacum sanctum, 32
Guapira discolor, 10
Gumbo-limbo, 22
Gymnanthes lucida, 40
Inkwood, 24
Jacquinia keyensis, 30
Jamaica Caper, 26
Jamaica Dogwood, 28
Joewood, 30
Krugiodendron ferreum, 6
Laguncularia racemosa, 68
Lignum Vitae, 32

Lysiloma latisiliquum, 74
Mahogany, 34
Manikara bahamensis, 70
Metopium toxiferum, 46
Milkbark, 36
Myrsine, 38
Oysterwood, 40
Paradise Tree, 42
Pigeon Plum, 44
Piscidia piscipula, 28
Pithecellobium keyense, 4
Poisonwood, 46
Rapanea punctata, 38
Red Mangrove, 48
Rhizophora mangle, 48
Sapindus saponaria, 58
Satinleaf, 50
Seagrape, 52
Seven-Year Apple, 54
Sideroxylon salicifolium,76
Sideroxylon foetidissimum, 16
Simarouba glauca, 42
Smooth Strongback, 56
Soapberry, 58
Spanish Stopper, 60
Spicewood, 62
Strangler Fig, 64
Sweet Acacia, 66
Swietenia mahagoni, 34
White Mangrove, 68
Wild Dilly, 70
Wild Lime, 72
Wild Tamarind, 74
Willow Bustic, 76
Zanthoxylum fagara, 72

Acknowledgements

Thank you to the following people who helped in the production of this book.

Janice Duquesnel from the Florida Department of Environmental Protection/Florida Park Service for botanical editorial and proofreading advice.
Susie Clock, Cynthia Edwards, Hazel Hans, Marysia Reid, Darin T. Robert, Jerry Sanders and Mali Wagner for their picky proofreading.
Nadja Hensen, Ann-Margaret Swary and Cheryl Smith at the *Key West Citizen*, my column editors.
Denise Knerr for creating a comprehensive 1996 *Lignum Vitae* tree brochure for the Garden Club.
Nathalie Breakstone for her inspiring cover design.
Neva Townsend for her artistic advice.
Kitty Somerville and Debby Crowley whose Monday morning Information Circles guided many columns and who wrote the grant that enabled this project to proceed.
Leah Brenner, Joan Langley and Reef Perkins in my Writing Group for their many wise and sometimes silly style suggestions. Special thanks to Reef Perkins for the title of the book.
Jeff Ware for computer and editing expertise.
The Key West Garden Club members who contributed their expertise to make this book possible.
The many Key West citizens who shared their expertise with me.

This book was partially funded by Southeast Florida Native Forest Restoration Program.

About the Author

Key West Garden Club's Robin Robinson, a Master Gardener, was previously a columnist for the Chicago Daily News. Princeton Features syndicated her children's column, "Robin's World," in over a hundred newspapers for over ten years. This book is part of a series developed by the Key West Garden Club, 1100 Atlantic Ave. Key West, Florida 33040 (305) 294-3210. For more information visit www.keywestgardenclub.com. The book was produced with funds from a grant from the Florida Division of Forestry funded by the US Forest Service.

QUICK ORDER FORM

Roots, Rocks and Rain: Native Trees of the Florida Keys
Key West Garden Club

Name _____

Address _____

City _____ **State**_____ **Zip**_____

Telephone _____

Email address _____

Order on the website: keywestgardenclub.com

For postal orders please send this form and check or money order to:

Key West Garden Club
P.O. Box 4131
Key West, Florida 33041

Price $19.95
Sales Tax: Please add $1.50 if shipped within Florida
Postage and Handling in US: $6.00 for first book,
$2.00 for each additional book